You Are a Miracle...
Waiting to Happen!

You Are a Miracle…
Waiting to Happen!

Ken Houts

Treasure House

An Imprint of
Destiny Image® Publishers, Inc.
P.O. Box 310
Shippensburg, PA 17257-0310

"For where your treasure is,
there will your heart be also." Matthew 6:21

ISBN 1-56043-260-8

For Worldwide Distribution
Printed in the U.S.A.

Ninth Printing: 2002   Tenth Printing: 2002

This book and all other Destiny Image, Revival Press,
MercyPlace, Fresh Bread, Destiny Image Fiction,
and Treasure House books are available
at Christian bookstores and distributors worldwide.

For a U.S. bookstore nearest you, call **1-800-722-6774**.
For more information on foreign distributors,
call **717-532-3040**.
Or reach us on the Internet: **www.destinyimage.com**

Dedication

To my wonderful wife Cheryl; without her faithfulness, courage, and loyalty I could not have entered into the destiny the Lord had for me. Also, to my three children, Joanna, Andrew, and Beth, who have taught me to love, laugh, and live.

Contents

Introduction

In 1986 the Lord gave me a six-hour vision revealing the Care Ministry to me. At the time I was on the staff of a megachurch of 4,000. It was a vision of the ministry of the believer meeting the needs of the people whom the Lord was working with. This ministry empowers the believer to grow into the ministry of the Spirit, and it equips churches to experience the harvest growth the Lord has ordained for them. The Care Ministry has changed the lives of Christians and churches throughout the world. This book is neither a theory nor a program, but actual ministry that occurs in churches every Sunday and in believers' lives every day. This is not a church growth program; it is a lifestyle of love that will empower readers to discover the miracles the Lord has prepared for them, and to lead scores of hurting people to the Lord.

Revival is breaking out in America today, and this ministry will empower you to release the revival the Lord has for you. As you read this book, you will learn how to enter the adventure of the ministry of the Spirit. You are a miracle waiting to happen because God is waiting to be a miracle through you. Enjoy this exciting adventure of discovering the miracle you are!

Values of the Care Ministry

1. The Ministry of the Believer

You are a miracle waiting to happen. The Lord is in each believer to meet the needs of others by the power of the Spirit and the love of God. The needs of the visitors, unchurched, and the unsaved cannot be met by church staff. Only by equipping the saints to do the work of ministry will the church gather the harvest.

2. Availability

My availability gives God opportunity to do a miracle through me. Miracles occur because of the grace and favor of God, and not man's natural or spiritual ability. Availability is the step of faith that gives God the opportunity to do what He wants to do: meet needs by the power of the Spirit.

3. Need Fulfillment Ministry

Visitors are not visitors; visitors are miracles disguised as needs. Jesus came to meet the needs of hurting humanity by the power of the love of God and the Spirit of God. The key to success is to find a need and fill it, find a hurt and heal it.

4. Relationships

Heartfelt needs are met through relationships. Relationships empower the Care member to meet the needs of others by first meeting the needs of those ministering. Loving relationships strengthen the Care member to meet needs and love bonds the visitor to the church.

5. Training

Training produces competence, competence produces confidence, and confidence produces success. Christians need more than the nurture of the Word to be effective ministers. *Ministry skills* training will equip the believer for effective need fulfillment ministry.

6. Team Ministry

Team Ministry produces multiplication by the power of the unity of the Spirit. Individual effort will not accomplish the purpose of the church. Team ministry releases the synergy of the Spirit by employing the gifts, strengths, and skills of each individual to become one on the Team. Interdependence on the Care Team releases each person to achieve the greatest effectiveness.

7. Discipleship

The goal of the Care Ministry is a disciple of Jesus Christ. The difference between a disciple and a decision is simply that a decision is invisible and a disciple is in church. A disciple is one who is initiated into the Kingdom of God, integrated into the relationships and ministry of the church, and owns the vision and values of the local church.

8. Vision

Vision produces faith, faith produces passion, and passion produces commitment. A fresh vision of the ministry of the believer, of the harvest, and of the relationships in the church will empower the Christian to experience the ministry the Lord has for them.

Chapter 1

This Is Your Day
to Become a Miracle!

Dorothy was excited and scared the first Sunday morning she ministered with her "Care Team." She told me, "Ken, I'm here, but I don't know what to do or say, and I'm scared!" I remembered passing a woman sitting alone in a row of 25 empty seats. I was sure she needed someone to care for her, so I pointed her out and said, "Dorothy, why don't you go talk to her?"

"What would I say?" Dorothy whispered. I gave her what I call "The Three Miracle-Working Questions." These questions help believers establish relationships and release God to do what only God can do: work miracles in the lives of hurting people. I told her to say, "Hi, my name is Dorothy. What's your name?" "How long have you been coming here?" and "Is there anything I can pray about with you?" Dorothy smiled and said, "I can do that!"

She went over to the visitor and said, "Hi, my name is Dorothy. What's your name?" The lady answered, "My name is Claudia." Dorothy smiled and asked, "Well, Claudia, how long have you been coming here?" Claudia answered, "I've been coming about four weeks." Then Dorothy improvised and asked, "Claudia, has anyone talked to you in the four weeks you've been coming here?" Dorothy was shocked when Claudia said, "No, no one has talked to me since I started attending here."

Claudia was one of the scores of hurting people who were "falling through the cracks" of this church of 4,000 people. The local church can be a tremendously lonely place when no one cares about you. In fact, Claudia had told herself, "If no one talks to me this Sunday, I'm not coming back." God had arranged a *divine appointment* for her with Dorothy.

Then Dorothy asked the miracle-working question, "Claudia, is there anything I can pray about with you?" Claudia began to cry, and she told Dorothy, "My husband is institutionalized with drug dependency—he wants a divorce; and my son is in satan worship. [Other than that, everything is fine!]" Claudia had come to church for four weeks with some big needs and pain, but no one cared until Dorothy asked to hear the pain.

This was the first time Dorothy had talked to anyone other than her friends at church, and she had encountered a real crisis! I had given her three simple questions and walked away. In that moment of crisis, God began to teach Dorothy a secret about ministry: divine-human cooperation. She *did what she could do* when she stepped out in faith and made herself *available*. That released God to *do what only God could do*—a miracle! Dorothy took Claudia's hands and prayed with her, sharing the pain, the tears, and the power of God with her. Then she sat with Claudia during the church service. At the end of the service, Claudia went forward to receive Jesus Christ as her Lord—with Dorothy at her side!

In the prayer room afterward, Claudia told her newfound friend, "Dorothy, I would have never gone forward if you had not loved me before church." Three months later, Claudia walked down the aisle with her husband when he received salvation; and three months after that, I prayed with her son. Claudia represents three miracles that happened because one woman named Dorothy made herself available to God. Everyone who wants to "be a miracle" in the lives of others should declare this confession of faith:

> My availability gives God opportunity
> to do a miracle through me.

I don't want to mislead you—Dorothy's church was a "friendly church." No one ever intended to ignore

Claudia. How about you? Do you have a "friendly" church? Frankly, I have *never* been to an unfriendly church because everybody thinks their church is friendly—just ask them! Most church leaders and members believe their church is "friendly" because the slim 10 percent of the visitors who become members usually tell them how friendly the church was to them. The real question is: "What about the 90 percent who left your friendly church and never came back?"

The Pastor's Nightmare

In the typical "friendly" church, Frank and Sally Visitor get a warm handshake and a nice seat for the service. Afterward, four or five people may go up to Frank and Sally and say, "Hi, how are you doing? Hope to see you next week." The attention makes them feel important, so Frank says to Sally on the way out, "This sure is a friendly church. Let's go back next week." The following week, Frank and Sally Visitor are greeted with, "Hi, how are you doing? Hope to see you next week."

Two months later, do you know what they're getting? "Hi, how are you doing? Hope to see you next week." Four months later, they are still getting the same "friendly" greeting, but one Sunday Frank asks Sally, "Honey, do you know anyone at church?" She says, "No, but it sure is a friendly church." Frank concludes, "Well, if you don't know anyone and I don't know anyone, maybe we should go to a church where we can get to know somebody." Next week, they are gone *searching for some friends.*

If they do come back one last time, the "friendly" church gives them their best: "Sure is good to see you. Hope to see you next week." Then they are gone. Two months later, after one or two greeters vaguely realize they are gone, they call them names like "steeple chasers," "church hoppers," "cruisamatics," "church flakes," and "uncommitted," with the epitaph, "Well, I guess Frank and Sally just didn't have the capacity to be committed like we do." We often blame visitors for not feeling loved, and belittle the harvest God sends to us. Visitors aren't the problem—we are!

The Church We *Didn't* Join

The relational principle, "You only have one chance to make a first impression," has application to visitors. Church growth studies have found visitors make up their minds in the first eleven minutes if they are not coming back to a church. The way we treat (or do *not* treat) visitors often tells them they are not really important to us and our church. I experienced this firsthand one time when my family was searching for a church home. I had a week off from my traveling schedule, so we attended the second service of a prospective church home because they had a class for teenagers.

When we walked through the door, no one greeted us or directed us to the area where the teen class met. When

I asked a woman who was taking names for the nursery where the teenage class was located, she said, "I don't know, but I think it's down that way." That information wasn't particularly helpful since there was only one doorway leading from the foyer.

We came upon a mass of people, and I was hoping someone would see the lost look on my face and ask us if we needed some help; but we were being ignored. Now, it is hard to ignore my family. I'm 6' 1", my son is also 6' 1", a daughter is 5' 10", and another daugther is 5' 9 1/2", and my wife is not short either. We are a hard family to ignore, but this crowd of church folks was successfully ignoring my entire family.

As we worked our way through the insensitive crowd of good church folk ignoring my family, I felt like my family and I were unimportant to that church. I did not feel like they cared about my family. They convinced me by their lack of ministry to my family that they did not care about us becoming part of their church. Of course, you could ask the question, "Should you have those feelings just walking down the hall not knowing where you were going in the crowd?" I do not know what I *should have felt* as a visitor and guest at that church, but I can tell you my *actual* feelings intensified.

We managed to walk through scores of people, and not one person said anything to us, even though I was attempting to make eye contact with someone. On the other side of the crowd we met Dan, one of my wife's friends, and the primary relationship that brought us there. I felt so glad to see him! He was an elder in the church, and he would certainly know where the class was located for my children.

I said, "Dan, where's the class for the teenagers?" He lamely responded, "I don't know, but I think it's down that way." He did not offer to help; he just went on his way. I am sure he had some church business to attend to.

When we finally found the teens' room, my children turned their backs to the door and acted like they wouldn't go in. As you know, teenagers don't like to endure new situations and strangers, and my children did not really want to go into that room full of strange kids.

I ignored their pleading eyes and said, "Well, go into the class now. We came here to the second service just for you to attend the class." My son, who respects and loves me, said, "Dad, we don't want to go into this class." My two teenage daughters were letting him be the spokesman for their mutiny. He obviously felt the lack of care the church had given us up to this point, and he did not want to experience any more.

I said, "I understand, but we came here for you to go to this class and you are going to this class." This conversation lasted for three to four minutes, and during this time teenagers were entering the room, looking at my children, ignoring them, and going into the class without saying a word. Every time a teen walked by without helping me, I got more frustrated. Finally I said, "Look, get in the class now!" So my teenagers entered the class with joy and anticipation. I knew they would really enjoy the class now.

By this time I had a high level of frustration from the continued absence of ministry to my family. Not surprisingly, no one said anything to us on the way to the sanctuary. In the sanctuary, no one said anything to us until the "greet-someone-next-to-you" segment in the liturgy. Two people talked to us: our friend the elder, and a single man who had been there for six months, who didn't know anyone either. Right then I said to myself, "I'm not coming back to this church again."

We had sung one song, and my mind was made up. I can't remember anything the pastor said, but it wasn't good enough to overcome all the negative communication I had received since I walked in the door. That church convinced me that neither I nor my family was important to them. They convinced me that they did not care about my children needing a Christian youth group. They convinced me that they were an unfriendly church. They persuaded me not to come back.

How many churches every week persuade visitors that they are not important, that no one cares about them, and that their needs are not the concern of the church? How many people walked out of the doors of your church last year, convinced you did not care for them? It is all rooted in attitudes of the heart.

Granddad's Pew

I grew up in a church where my granddad was a deacon, and he had his "place" in the sanctuary. It was the third pew back on the left. For more than 40 years, he sat there every time the doors were open! That pew was conformed to my granddaddy's body shape. One Sunday, some visitors sat in his place. Boy, was he upset! "They sat in my place," he complained. Granddaddy did not enjoy the church service. In fact, it wasn't "church" as far as he was concerned because he wasn't in his place. My granddaddy was guilty of being a human creature of habit. Many churches and good church people lose sight of the "big picture" of the harvest when somebody sits squarely in the middle of their smaller "comfort" picture. Growth always brings change! Maybe that is why so many churches seem to fight success and growth so stubbornly!

How Do You Spell Relief?

When Peter and Mona attended a church in Florida for the first time, Peter had a headache. He was not looking forward to enduring the church service in pain, and he expected the usual "visitor experience" consisting of superficial contacts with church members. Peter and Mona didn't know it, but they were about to experience a miracle through the church's brand-new "Care Ministry."

John came to church prepared for an "adventure" in the Spirit of God—he came prepared to meet needs as a Care minister. He approached Peter and Mona in the foyer before they were seated. As they talked, John asked, "Is there anything I can pray about with you?" Peter joked, "Yeah, I've got this headache..." John believed God would meet that need, so he asked, "Can I pray for your headache?" When John prayed, the Lord touched Peter and the headache left.

Peter was so excited about being touched by God in the church foyer—even before the service began! Peter and Mona became "second-time attenders" when they came to the Sunday night service. They had found a church that *cared*! In the first few minutes of their first visit, they had found a friend who prayed with them for their *needs* to be met.

Fast Lane in the Foyer

Most people think you "get to know" other Christians by talking to other members in the foyer. My dad always went to church 15 minutes early so he could "fellowship in the foyer" with Brother Harris. Every Sunday morning and evening, and Wednesday night, we went to church early to "fellowship in the foyer." Brother Houts and Brother Harris always "fellowshipped" in the foyer, talking about the Kansas City Royals and the Kansas City Chiefs. They would go to Sunday school, then go to the sanctuary for the sermon, and then hurry back to the foyer to "fellowship" some more. We even went to monthly fellowship dinners and other "fellowship" activities.

The problem is that we never knew Brother Harris had been laid off, and we never knew about his family struggles or victories. The fact is that we really didn't have a *relationship* with Brother Harris. Why? You can't develop relationships in the foyer.

Only God really knows how many "miracles" walk through your church doors disguised as needs. We don't need to enlarge our professional church staff or add more buildings. The solution is sitting in the pews! It is time for the Church to encounter the "Ezekiel experience." There are millions of "Dorothys" and "Brother Johns" who long to become a "miracle" in someone's life! In fact, *this is your day to become a miracle!*

Chapter 2

You Are a Miracle in God's Army!

Just before the church service began, Dwight walked up to a lady he had never met before. He asked her if there was anything he could pray about with her, and she told him that she was sick. As Dwight began to pray with her, he also sensed that she was discouraged. He prayed against the discouragement in the name of Jesus. Tears began to stream down the woman's face as she said, "God sent you to me, didn't He?"

Dwight had a "divine appointment" that morning. There are divine appointments in your church every time the doors open because *people* come to church when they *are troubled*. They are looking for someone who will love them, pray with them, and minister to them.

*So I prophesied as He commanded me, and the breath
came into them, and they came to life, and stood on
their feet, an **exceedingly great army** (Ezekiel
37:10).*

God has purposed that in the last days, He will have
an army of Spirit-filled believers meeting the needs of
hurting people! But don't you know that every time
God has a purpose to accomplish in the earth, He always has a problem to overcome? Let's find out what
the problem is:

*The hand of the Lord was upon me, and He brought
me out by the Spirit of the Lord and set me down in the
middle of the valley; and it was full of bones. And He
caused me to pass among them round about, and behold, there were very many on the surface of the valley;
and lo, **they were very dry** (Ezekiel 37:1-2).*

Now who do you think those bones were? I minister
in churches all across America, and do you know what
I find in every church? *Dry bones!* We are the dry bones;
good church folk are the bones. "We are da bones, we
are dry, and we are da problem!" God wants all of us to
be living miracles meeting needs. We don't want to be
dry, but we are!

The "Last Days" Army of God

You are doing everything you know to do to be a
good Christian. You go to church every week (sometimes *three* times a week). You pray and read God's

Word, but you are still dry. Now the "dry bones" are not bad folk at all. In fact, most of the dry bones I find are really good church folk!

The good news is that every time you have a problem, God has a promise. God has a promise for every Christian who feels dry! In fact, God cannot do a miracle in your life unless you have a problem! He has a miracle in His hand, and He can't do a miracle without a need.

And He said to me, "Son of man, can these bones live?" And I answered, "O Lord God, Thou knowest." Again He said to me, "Prophesy over these bones, and say to them, 'O dry bones, hear the word of the Lord.' Thus says the Lord God to these bones, 'Behold, I will cause breath [of My Spirit] *to enter you that you may come to life' "* (Ezekiel 37:3-5).

I have a promise from God for you today! God says, "I will cause breath [of My Spirit] to enter you that you may come to life." God has a fresh move of the Spirit for you! Fresh anointing comes from a fresh vision. God wants you to have a fresh vision of your ministry and of yourself. The Care Ministry will give you that fresh vision of your ministry and anointing.

God Needs You!

God has a promise for every dry bone in the Church today. He wants you to have a fresh move of the Spirit! He's not condemning you, and He's not mad at you for being dry. He has a promise for you: "Thus says the Lord God to these bones, 'Behold, I will cause breath [of My Spirit] to enter you that you may come to life' " (Ezek. 37:5).

Many Christians have asked me, "Ken, we want God's fresh wind of the Spirit to blow over us! What do we do?" They are saved and go to church regularly, yet they are still dry. Perhaps the problem is that the move of the Spirit is supposed to come from doing something *other* than simply going to church meetings!

Do you want a fresh anointing from God? All you have to do is learn how to cooperate with the Lord, and you will be able to do what He has always wanted to do through you: *meet the needs* of others and *do miracles* through you!

A miracle is when a *need meets its solution*. A miracle is a *divine appointment*, when a person with pain meets a person with the power of God within! *You are a miracle waiting to happen* because you have God inside you, and He is waiting to *meet someone's needs* through you!

The Care Ministry grew out of the vision God gave us to help "ordinary Christians" step into the extraordinary by experiencing *times of refreshing* from the move of the Spirit! God wants to refresh you and move upon you with a fresh anointing, but you will have to be trained to do the ministry. You are about to discover how to have a fresh anointing!

Four Symptoms of a Dry Bone

There are four symptoms of "dry bones." If these symptoms apply to you, then you're suffering from spiritual dryness, and it is time to change. If you are a dry bone, then God is giving you a choice right now: You can remain "good church folk" and go to church two or three times a week, or you can become part of the miracle-working army of God meeting the needs of people in pain! If you choose to change, then pray this prayer aloud:

God, You want me to have a fresh move of the Spirit. I don't want to be a dry bone. I want to be in the army of God. If these symptoms apply to my life, I'm going to change.

Number One: You are spiritually stagnant if your Christian walk hasn't changed much. You just haven't grown much. You don't sense the flow of the Spirit like you used to, and your prayers don't seem that effective. You don't get much out of God's Word anymore. You sense there is more to your Christian life, but you don't know what it is.

There is an analogy of this condition in the two seas of Israel: the Dead Sea and the Sea of Galilee. I was in Israel a few years ago and stopped at the Dead Sea. When we walked around the bus, it hit us. It stunk. Do you know why it stunk? It was dead. It was dead all around the sea, and dead in the sea—it was dead. People got out of the bus and got all excited about seeing something dead. "Oh, look! The Dead Sea!" they cried. I said, "Yeah, it's dead all right. I want to see something that's *alive!*"

We got back into the bus and drove up to Tiberias, on the Sea of Galilee. It is one of the most beautiful places you could ever see. The Sea of Galilee is alive—it has life all around it. Thousands of people are fed from the life within the Sea of Galilee. *There is only one difference between the Sea of Galilee and the Dead Sea.* The Sea of Galilee has both an inlet and an outlet, but *the Dead Sea only has an inlet.*

The Dead Sea is just like a lot of us good church folks. You come to church after an awfully hard week. In fact, it has been such a hard week that you think the devil himself has come out of hell to torment you. You drag into church thinking, "I hope the choir has a good song today. I hope the pastor has a good word today—boy, do I need it."

Sure enough, the worship is great, and it blesses you. The pastor gives you a word that encourages you and builds you up. When you're all filled up, you waddle out of church and go home to take a nap! You come back Sunday night, get all filled up again, and waddle home to bed.

What happens when all you do is eat and eat, but never exercise? You get fat. God wants a "lean, mean, fighting machine," but what He gets is a fat church: "My name is Jimmy, so gimme, gimme, gimme."

We "evaluate" church by *what we get.* "What did you *get out of* church today?" Church isn't just a place to get; it is a place to *give!* We are spiritually stagnant because all we do is get, get, get. The Spirit only moves on us after *we* move! Sitting and getting does not release God's Spirit.

Number Two: Your "comfort zone" lies in living a life that is *less* than the life God created you to live! You have not released or enjoyed the gifts, skills, talents, life, and abilities God has put in you. The potential in you has not been released! Can you sense there is more in you than you are experiencing right now? As long as you stay in your comfort zone, *you will never know why you were saved!* You will never enter into your redeemed destiny.

Jesus did not die to give you "fire insurance"! He died so you could know your redeemed destiny. I wanted to know why God looked down from Heaven and said, "I want Ken Houts!" I discovered that He didn't just save me so I could go to Heaven; He saved me because He had *invested in me!* He has invested His divine gifts, abilities, skills, and abundant life in you, too, and *He wants a return on His investment!*

I had been pastoring successfully for 17 years when God revealed the Care Ministry to me. Everyone at the church of 4,000 liked me and God was blessing the ministry. Then I read something in God's Book about Peter walking on the water, and I "felt a breath blowing over my bones…."

Peter said, "Lord, if it is You, command me to come to You on the water" (Mt. 14:28b). Jesus only said one word: "Come!" Peter looked down at the churning water and dared to believe he could do what no fisherman had ever done before! Now about that time, "Doubting Thomas" began to tell anyone who would listen, "He's not going to make it. He can't walk on water. He's going to sink." When God wants you to be a "water-walker," doubt will always try to stop you! Peter looked at Jesus and leapt into the sea anyway! Instead of sinking like he had thousands of times before, a miracle happened! Peter was a "water-walker"! His faith was the "assurance of things hoped for" that held him above the waves!

God told me, "Ken, that boat is the *boat of your security*; and the water is the *water of opportunity*!" Don't look for Jesus in the boat of your security; you will find Him on the water of opportunity. You will have to step out of the boat of your security and walk on the water of opportunity to meet Jesus!

I told a friend about the Care Ministry vision and asked him if he thought it would work in other churches. My friend Don jumped past my comfort zone and pushed me into the realm of faith when he said, "Ken, you'll never know *unless you try it.*"

Right then, God said, "Ken, get out of your boat." You are in the same situation right now: You'll never know why you were saved or experience the miracles God has for you unless you get out of your boat. Why should you take the chance of getting out of your boat? Because God wants to reward you!

The Bible says, "And without faith it is *hard* to please God." Is that what Hebrews 11:6 says? No, but that is the way a lot of Christians read it! Many Christians think, "If I go to church, am a nice person, read my Bible, pray, and live a holy life, I'll please God." That is not what the Bible says. God's Word says, "And without *faith* it is *impossible* to please Him!" (Heb. 11:6a) You cannot please God in the boat of your securities. You must come to God in *faith.*

What is faith? "Now faith is the assurance of things hoped for, the conviction of things not seen" (Heb. 11:1). Faith is the substance of hope. Without hope there is no need for faith. Many Christians have *lost hope* for the future. They have been disappointed so many times that they don't want to take the risk of hoping again.

Hope is an "optimistic expectancy of good." You cannot be a pessimistic Christian; it is a contradiction in terms. If you are a Christian, you are an *optimist!*

Psychologists placed a pessimistic boy in a room full of toys, and when they returned a few minutes later, the boy had scattered the toys all over the room. He was sitting in the middle of the floor with a pout on his face. When they asked him what was wrong, the pessimistic boy said, "There's just nothing to do!"

Then they placed an optimistic boy in a room that contained nothing but a large pile of horse manure. When they returned a few minutes later, the optimistic boy was digging through the middle of that pile of manure, throwing manure out onto the floor. The psychologists ran into the room and asked, "What are you doing?" The optimistic boy said, "With this much manure, *there's got to be a pony in here somewhere!*"

I have some good news for you—God's got a pony for you! Too many Christians only see the pile, and that is all they talk about. They never look for "the pony." God is your Rewarder! All you have to do is abandon your boat of security, leave your comfort zone, and answer His call to receive your reward. The devil wants to steal your miracle and leave you with a pile of horse manure, but God has a pony for you!

Number Three: You are spiritually barren and nonproductive if you have not seen anyone saved through your personal ministry recently! Would you agree that since statistics indicate that 95 percent of all Christians in America today are barren, then the Church is under a curse of barrenness? Are you ready to break the curse of barrenness and glorify God by your fruitfulness?

A spiritual disease is rampant in the Church. I see it in different churches every week, and I spot this disease with a very simple diagnostic question: "Have you been saved for five years or longer?" If you have, then I am sorry to tell you that you have a spiritual disease that is causing your barrenness. It's a good thing you are reading this book, or you would never know you had this disease! Have you heard of the Greek word *koinonia*? It means "Christian fellowship," or Christians sharing the common life of the Lord.

This kind of fellowship is great until you get diseased. You have a spiritual disease that grows when Christians have only Christian friends. I call it "koinonitis." There are three layers of koinonitis that are insulating you from the very people who need you the most. These three layers of insulation will keep you barren until Jesus comes back.

The first cause of spiritual barrenness is this: You have an attitude! "An attitude?! I don't have an attitude; I'm a good Christian!" But you do have an attitude. You don't like to be around unbelievers because they are not your kind of people. After all, they smoke, they drink, they tell dirty jokes, they cuss all the time, and they are mean. Most Christians think, "I would rather be around my Christian brothers and sisters than be around those kinds of people—I might get sin on me." The Bible says, "Greater is He who is in you than he who is in the world" (1 Jn. 4:4b). Instead of being afraid of getting sin on us, it's time for the world to be afraid of us getting God on them! We have insulated ourselves from the very people who need God the most, so we are barren because we don't like to be around those kinds of people.

The second cause of barrenness is this: All our activities are Christian activities. We don't do anything with unbelievers. We have Christian dinners, then Christian potlucks, another Christian dinner, then we have a Christian seminar, then another Christian potluck, then another Christian dinner. Everything we do is Christian, and we don't do anything with unbelievers.

One summer during the 17 years I pastored, some church members asked if we would sponsor a team in the co-ed softball church league. I said, "That's fine, but you've got to have some unbelievers on the team." They went out, got some unbelievers, and put them on the team. We were the only team in the league that had people cussing during the game! We were the only team in the league that had people smoking and drinking a brewskie after the game. And praise God, we were also the only team that had four people saved before the season was over! Those unbelievers got around us and liked us. Do you know why they liked us? God was inside us. When they got around us, they got around God.

The third cause of barrenness is this: All your friends are Christian. You don't have any unbelieving friends. The only way to solve that problem is to go out and get an unbelieving friend. Just go up to some unbeliever and say, "All my friends are Christians; I don't have an unbelieving friend. I need an unbelieving friend."

But how do you minister to unbelievers? Don't drag them to church, because if church were relevant to them, they would be there. You must *earn the right* to invite them to church. You begin by having fun with them. Every woman I know loves to go to the mall, and the only ones who say they don't are the ones who don't have any money (and every man knows that doesn't stop a woman from going to the mall). Every man I know loves to have fun either by hunting, fishing, golfing, or going to ball games.

Ministry begins by being yourself and having fun. Some Saturday morning, your wife will get up and declare, "Honey, I'm going to the mall all day today—it's my *ministry*!" Or your husband will say, "I'm going to be ministering today—on the golf course." What do you do with unbelievers? Simply go have fun with them. It's a tough job, but someone has got to do it! Christians ask me, "What if they ask me a question I don't know the answer to, like, 'How many angels fit on the head of a needle?' What am I going to say to them?"

People don't care how much you know until they know how much you care! People are not looking for answers; they are looking for relationships of love and care. We are barren because we have isolated ourselves from the very people who need the love of God inside us. It's time to break out of our insulation of barrenness and be fruitful for God!

Number Four: You have too many members in church! I know you are thinking, "We have too many members? I thought we were supposed to want more members!" Let me ask you some questions. Do you consider the full-time pastoral staff to be the *ministers* of the church, and the attenders the members? The staff will get you born, married, and buried, and everything else in between.

The attitude of the church members is, "I am a member of the church, so I deserve the ministry of the pastor. I may not tithe, but I do tip." (Tipping is giving the loose change in your pocket.) "Being a member of the church entitles me to receive the ministry of the pastor and staff."

Or are the pastors the equippers of the believers, empowering them to minister to the needs of others? The Bible says Jesus Christ gave us pastors "for the equipping of the saints for the work of service [ministry]" (Eph 4:12a). Your pastor is to not only meet your needs, but also train you to meet the needs of others.

Why did God save you to minister? There are too many needs for only the pastor to care for. There are even too many needs for the elder board or deacon board to care for! They can't do it, even if you don't include the needs of first-time attenders who visit every week!

Did Jesus say, "And these signs will acompany *the pastor*" in Mark 16:17? No? Then surely "...these signs will accompany the *board*." No? Then "...these signs will accompany the *evangelist*." No? Jesus said, "And these signs will accompany *those who have believed!*" The greatest sign that you are a believer in Jesus Christ is that you have made disciples of Christ too.

God has miracles for *everyone who believes*. If you are a *believer* in Jesus Christ, then God has *ordained miracles* for you and through you! Can you believe that God is big enough to handle your problems—and someone else's problems—through you? Don't wait until your life is "problem free" to minister. Just *trust God* to be big enough *in you!*

It is your destiny to meet needs, experience miracles, and destroy the works of the devil every day, and every time you go to church—through the *divine appointments* of God. It is God who matches up a person in pain with a person with His power! If you have God in you, then you are a person with God's power!

There were divine appointments in church last week because there were people hurting in church last week!

I can guarantee you there will be divine appointments in church this week! The question is this: *Will these appointments be made or broken?*

The ministry of Jesus Christ was a "need-fulfillment ministry." He said He had come to "...heal the broken-hearted, to preach deliverance to the captives..." (Lk. 4:18 KJV). Jesus came to meet needs. If the Church is going to be the Church, then we must meet needs through the people as well as through the pulpit!

Visitors are not visitors; they are miracles disguised as needs. They each come to church with one question: "Can you meet my needs?" They are need-driven to find God. The church that meets their needs will be the church that grows. When I implement the Care Ministry into a local church, *I give an altar call for ministry.* Then I have a brief meeting with everyone who wants to be part of God's army of need-meeting ministers. A woman named Betty was going to one of these meetings, but as she explained to me later, "The Holy Spirit arrested me and led me over to one of the visitors. Just as you said, Ken, she came to church with a big need. I prayed with her, and we both cried for joy."

"God Touched Somebody Through Me!"

Betty told me, "I don't know what it did for her, but I know what it did for me!" Betty was excited because she saw God touch the needs of someone *through her*! She suddenly sensed a fresh move of the Spirit in her life! She began to realize for the first time in her life that God *did have a ministry for her*. She experienced a fresh anointing.

You can have the same experience as Betty if you will make yourself available to God and enter into the purposes of God for your life. You don't have to go to Africa to be in God's army; you can do the ministry right in your own church! There are needs "wanting to become miracles" every week in church.

There is a choice for you to make: Either continue being a good churchgoer who goes to church to get blessed and go to Heaven; or become part of the army of God and fulfill your redeemed destiny! When God saved you, He had already ordained miracles for you. If you want God to use you, then this is your time for miracles!

Take the first step toward your destiny and pray this prayer before you read any further:

Father, I thank You for loving me enough to save me. I thank You that I have a redeemed destiny. I don't want to miss any more miracles. I don't want to miss any more "divine appointments" You have for me. I repent of being spiritually stagnant. I want to go on in You. I want to grow into all of the ministry of the Spirit You have for me. There are gifts, talents, skills, strengths, ministry, and life hidden inside of me. To-day, I want to get out of my boat of security and walk

*on the water of opportunity! I want to see the miracles
You have for me. Today, I walk by faith and not by
sight. Today, I walk in the boldness of faith.*

*Father, I haven't been fruitful in a long time, but I
want to bear much fruit and glorify Your name. Today,
I make myself available to tell people about Jesus.
There are too many needs for the staff to care for, so I
give myself to You today to meet the needs of the hurting people You bring to my church. I ask You to show
me how I can meet those needs.*

*I no longer want to be a member just receiving the
blessings; I choose this day to be part of the army of
God, and to be a blessing to all those around me. I will
look for "divine appointments" in my life—every day.
I am a miracle waiting to happen. Together we can destroy the works of the devil. I pray these things in the
name of Jesus. Amen.*

As you read the rest of this book, it will help equip
you to meet the needs of hurting people in your life—
not just those at church, but people in the grocery
store, at work, and wherever you find a need. You are
now ready to begin the adventure of the supernatural
army of God!

Every time you go to a church service or start a new day,
you walk right past people who are *waiting on someone
like you* to touch them with the love of God! They are

looking for someone who can help them experience the miracle God has ordained for them!

A miracle is waiting for you today! This is the day you could become the miracle *God saved you to be.* He has called you to a future of "divine appointments" and exciting ministry! Now is the time to discover God's pattern to find the miracles of ministry He has for you. I do believe that *you are a miracle waiting to happen!*

Chapter 3

Visitors Are Miracles Disguised as Needs

Darrell and Mary went to church ready and available to God for the ministry of the Spirit. They greeted Sam and Jennifer after church because they had received their visitors' card during the Team Meeting at the end of the announcements. As Darrell and Mary listened to Sam and Jennifer, the visitors began to realize the only reason Darrell and Mary were talking to them was to meet their need. That's when Sam opened up.

"We haven't been in church in years," Sam said, "and the only reason we are here today is because we were in jail last night." Sam watched Darrell and Mary's reaction, and when they didn't flinch, he continued the story. "We wanted to have a good time last night, so we were wanting to get some 'recreational drugs.' We don't smoke pot more than a couple times a year, but this time we bought some—from an undercover agent. The police confiscated my new Jeep as evidence because it had drug paraphernalia in it, so now we don't have transportation. We have to go to court, and our whole life is a mess."

"We Came Hoping Someone Would Care"

That's when Jennifer said, "I told him this morning what we needed to do was get to church today! One of my friends told me about this church, and how you can get help here. We came hoping someone would care about us—even though we did drugs and got busted." Darrell and Mary listened, cared, and asked them if they really wanted to get their lives straightened out.

Sam said, "I've been putting this off long enough. Last night got my attention." That's when Darrell knew he could pray with them to receive Jesus Christ. He asked them if they had ever received Jesus as their Lord, and they both said no. Then he led them in the sinner's prayer and made an appointment to see them the next night.

As Darrell and Mary drove to keep the appointment the following night, they knew from the information on the "First-Time Attender Prayer Request Card" that Sam and Jennifer had two different last names and only one address, which indicated they were probably unmarried and living together. Darrell knew he had to address the issue in love and grace, but that it still needed to be confronted. When they arrived, Sam and Jennifer were excited about how their lives had changed in just two days.

Then Jennifer volunteered, "Darrell, Sam and I have been talking about our life together, and we feel like we need to get married." Isn't God good? The Holy Spirit convicted them and gently led these new converts to repent—without Darrell saying anything.

Sam said, "We would like to have a church wedding, but we don't know where we could do it or who would perform the ceremony." Darrell told them they could have the ceremony at the church. Mary volunteered to play the piano, and Darrell said one of the pastors would probably be happy to officiate. Jennifer exclaimed, "The church would do all that for us?" Darrell assured her there would be no problem in arranging it. Then Sam revealed a big need. "Darrell, I don't have a friend who would stand with me in the ceremony as my best man." Darrell quickly said, "Sam, I would be happy to stand with you in your wedding." Sam and Jennifer hugged Darrell and Mary, and cried with them in their excitement about how dramatically their lives had changed in just a few short days. Sam and Jennifer agreed to live apart until the wedding day.

Sam Got Married in Darrell's Suit

At the wedding ceremony, Darrell was standing in his place in the church chapel waiting for Sam. When the groom walked down the aisle, Darrell recognized his suit. (You see, Darrell had given a number of his suits to Frank, who was a member of the Care Group. Frank and Sam had also become good friends, and Sam told Frank that he didn't have a suit for the wedding. Frank said, "I've got plenty! Darrell gave me some of his suits so I could minister in the Care Ministry.") Sam got married in a suit Darrell had given to him (in partnership with Frank), *and* his life was changed by the Lord that Darrell had introduced him to!

Darrell and Mary destroyed the works of the devil and fulfilled the Great Commission—in their local church! They did not go to the inner city (although that is good), and they did not go to Africa (that is also good); they went to church and *ministered to the needs of the visitors!*

> Visitors are not visitors—
> visitors are miracles disguised as needs.

Visitors all come to church with one question: *"Can you meet my needs?"* You can fulfill the Great Commission—in church. You can destroy the works of the devil—in church. You can be fruitful and glorify God—in church. How? God brings a harvest to church every week! All you have to do is *find a need and fill it, and find a hurt and heal it.* To find the miracles, you must know what the needs are.

A miracle takes place when a need meets the solution. Visitors are miracles disguised as needs because they come to church yearning for their needs to be met, not to look for a church home! If you want to discover the miracles in your church every week, discover the condition of the visitors who come to your church. When you know their condition or individual problems, you will have compassion.

Ministry Must Be Moved by Compassion

Compassion is a "sympathetic consciousness of others' distress together with a desire to alleviate it."[1] It is also the relational skill to see beyond the external and feel the internal. In the Care Ministry, you view people differently—you view them with compassion. You don't look at their ties, suits, dresses, hats, shoes, or purses. You don't care what they have or don't have. What you care about is their soul.

I believe compassion is a relational skill because, like other skills, it can be *learned.* The objective of Care Ministry is to feel what others feel, and to give ourselves to meet their need through Christ. Once we learn to understand the pain, we will quickly release the power of the Spirit of God to meet the need. The prophet Ezekiel can help us understand the pain of the "first-time attenders" with this prophetic declaration of God:

> *My flock wandered through all the mountains and on every high hill, and My flock was scattered over all the surface of the earth; and there was no one to search or seek for them* (Ezekiel 34:6).

In the Old Testament, people worshiped on the mountains and high hills. This passage is a picture of people wandering from one mountaintop to another looking for God. If there were ever a picture of the world today, this is it! People are going from one church to another looking for God, looking for somebody to love them, yet they are scattered. Visitors are not visitors—they are *scattered sheep* that belong to God. You have the heart and compassion of God, or you would not be reading this book.

Three Keys to Meeting Needs

There are three keys to meeting the needs of visitors that will also apply to virtually every other situation involving the needs of people.

1. *Ministry must be personal.* Personal ministry will have greater impact on hurting people than pulpit ministry can. One pastor told me about Cheryl, who came into his office on a Tuesday and said, "Pastor, I want to become part of the church because I enjoyed Sunday night service so

much." He asked her if she enjoyed his message, thinking that was the reason she was going to become part of the church.

She said, "Well, I did enjoy your message, but it wasn't your message that made me want to be part of the church. The reason I want to be part of your church," Cheryl continued, "is because after church, you had everybody greet somebody and then take hold of their hands and pray for them." Then she revealed her need: "I came to church on Sunday night because on Saturday morning, my husband cleaned out my house and left me with three kids.

"I needed to be touched," she told the surprised pastor, "not just by God, but by somebody." Finally she revealed her motivation for membership: "One of the women in your church came over and held my hand, and she began to pray for me. She prayed for my needs and she touched me. That's why I'm going to be a member of this church." The woman talked about personal care, personal ministry, and personal involvement. First-time attenders don't merely need a message; they need ministry. They don't necessarily come looking for a pastor; they need a friend.

2. *Ministry must meet needs.* Where there is no need, there is no ministry. The first step to meet a need

is to discover and understand it. The process of discovering the needs of the visitors and ministering to those needs is the exciting ministry of the Spirit. Although techniques and information will help, only the Spirit of God can truly empower you to meet the needs of other people.

3. *Ministry must be relational.* Become their friend. We've found that visitors need to develop seven friendships in the church within six months, or they are out the back door! *The beginning of all ministry is becoming a visitor's friend the first Sunday he attends.*

Seven Conditions of Hurting Sheep

"Visitor" is a non-biblical term. When we call somebody a visitor, that means we do not feel we have a responsibility for that person's well-being. Some may even begin to criticize the people who come to the church looking for God! There are seven conditions we must learn to recognize in hurting sheep who walk through the door and into our lives.

1. *They are discouraged with their life.* People come to church because they have problems that seem unsolvable. They have problems with their boss, their spouse, and their kids. They walk in unhappy, discouraged, or depressed, thinking, "Surely, there is something better than the life I am living now!" They don't really know if God

can help them because they believe more in their problems than they believe in God.

2. *They have no spiritual direction.* They are wandering from one mountaintop to another with no spiritual direction. Your care and love is a very significant element in their lives for finding God. They're looking for some external "sign" that this church is the place God wants them. The number one thing they are looking for is a people who will love them and help them meet their needs; but they have no direction, and they don't know what God wants them to do.

3. *They are lonely.* Visitors are often afraid you wouldn't like them if you knew "what they were really like." They have a hard time liking themselves because all they can see are their problems, sins, and mistakes. They don't know why someone like you would like them. They enter the church wondering, "Will these people care about me, and love me the way I am?"

Anyone who has moved to your city within the past 24 months does not have a friend. That is why it is so important to ask people who come to your church, "How long have you lived here?" If they say anything less than 24 months, then they are looking for a friend, since it takes an average of two years to make friends in a new city. (And there are many who have been going to your church for two years or more *who still need a friend!*)

4. *They are weak and vulnerable.* The weight of sin or past mistakes may make them feel weak and spiritually vulnerable. If they do not get help when they come, not only will they not come back, but they often conclude God does not care about them, and quit church altogether!

5. *They are hurt and wounded.* Many visitors have been betrayed, rejected, criticized, put down, and made to feel worthless. They question their own value, and desperately need your acceptance, attention, and ministry to help them feel valuable. Over half of the first-time attenders who come to your church will have gone through a divorce or come from broken homes, and they will need love and attention.

Most people who leave one church and go to another have left because they got into a tiff, or somebody hurt or wounded them. They need solace from another part of the Church family. It may or may not be their fault—but it doesn't really matter! Pastors have said to me, "Well, people who leave one church and come to another *are going to bring their problems.*" I just ask them,

"Are you saying there are people who come to this church and *don't bring their problems?*"

Everybody who comes to your church brings his problems! Just because someone left another church to come to yours doesn't mean we are not to have compassion on that person. I'm telling you, he won't go back to the other church. He is hurt, wounded, and resentful. He doesn't think the people in the other church love him, so there is no way he is going to go back and work it out. Very few people have the fortitude to do that, and many times it isn't even wise.

We need to have enough faith to believe God can touch such people and heal them. Even if they were "troublemakers" in the other church, we still need to minister to them. I've had people give me trouble, and then go on to another church where they were the most wonderful people! Sure, it was frustrating as a pastor. I wanted to call the other pastor and "warn him" about my former troublemakers, but they were being "wonderful folk" over there! God can heal wounded hearts, but the army of God is the only army that "shoots their own wounded."

6. *They are condemned.* By reminding them every day about every mistake, every failure, and every sin they've ever committed, the devil has convinced many visitors that they are miserable *because they*

deserve to be miserable. He tells them all their misery is their fault. They believe the devil so much, they are not sure God would help them even if He could. "Why would God help somebody as bad as me?"

7. *They are spiritually hungry.* They are hungry for peace, they are hungry for God, they are hungry for what you have. You may think you need help, but if you have Jesus Christ in your life, then you have a whole lot more than they do if they are unsaved!

In one Care Ministry Seminar, I asked, "Which one of these seven conditions do you think people feel the most?" One guy in the back raised his hand and said, "I was a visitor in this church a month ago, and I felt all seven of them!" How are you going to get compassionate with people when you see these seven conditions? You must begin to pray.

Pray this prayer:

> *God, I want to feel when people are hungry, discouraged, lonely, confused, or vulnerable. I want to be able to feel what they feel, Lord. I want to be able to discern the needs of the people You bring to my church. In Jesus' name, amen.*

Visitors: Christian Myths and Heartfelt Needs

Many Christians don't want to reach out to visitors because of their misconceptions about visitors. In fact, many people still call visitors "strangers"! These "Christian myths" have caused countless "visitors" to leave our churches disillusioned about God and His Church. It is time to move past the myths into reality so God can meet needs through you!

It is true that every visitor comes through your church door with needs. Their deepest motivations, however, stem from four "universal heartfelt needs" that are nearly the opposite of what our "Christian myths" tell us! None of us is conscious of these needs, but we all know *when they are met*. When these needs are met, people feel like staying in your church. If you know how to overcome the myths to meet the heartfelt needs, then you will open the door wide for every "visitor" you encounter, and the "guests" will want to stay!

These are the "Christian Myths" that bind us, and the matching "Heartfelt Needs" that release God's compassion in us to meet needs:

Myth Number 1: *I'm just looking.* For some reason, we think people are motivated by "curiosity" to attend our church. These people aren't just looking for a church; *they are looking for God*, and for His *solutions to their needs*.

The Heartfelt Need: *They need to be accepted.* Every "first-time attender" feels out of place in a new church. As we noted earlier, they are wondering, "Do these people accept me just the way I am? Or will

I have to change to be accepted?" If they do not *feel accepted by you* because they look, talk, or act differently from you, they will not come back. This means you have lost all chance of ministering to them.

Myth Number 2: *I want to be left alone.* No, they *don't* want to be left alone. They want both *anonymity* and *attention* at the same time! In other words, no one wants an embarrassing label stuck on their lapel that says, "I'm a visitor." It makes them stick out and be different *in an uncomfortable way.* First-time attenders want to be like everybody else, but they also *want attention.* That's why they came to church.

The Heartfelt Need: *They need to belong.* You don't belong to a meeting. You don't belong to a building. You don't belong to a denomination or a fellowship. *You belong to people.* If the "first-time attender" does not have the relationships and friendships he needs, he will not stay. (Why should he?)

Myth Number 3: *I don't have any problems.* Some visitors may come to church looking better off than we are! They'll dress great, look great, drive a great car, and appear to have no problems. The fact remains that people go to church because they need God, and they need the kind of resources that *only God can provide.* Meanwhile, you are tempted to think, "Boy, those people don't need God; they're successful!" No, they are probably aching inside. You need the compassion of God to look beyond the external to the internal.

The Heartfelt Need: *They need to be needed.* Buildings don't need you. Pews don't need you. *People need you.* To belong, you must feel like someone in the church will miss you when you are gone, and that someone needs your love and friendship. That doesn't mean we should view "first-time attenders" only from the perspective of what they can do for the church. Only when the church first serves and meets the needs of "first-time attenders" will they become active, serving members of the church.

Myth Number 4: *Don't bother me.* Don't believe this lie of the enemy. Everyone wants love, attention, and care. If they wanted solitude, they certainly wouldn't head for the nearest church on Sunday morning.

The Heartfelt Need: *They need to feel important.* Do you like to be around people who don't think you are important? Of course not! Neither do "first-time attenders." The problem is that in most churches, "first-time attenders" are not *the important people* in the church—and they can feel it! If you do not know how to make "first-time attenders" feel important the first Sunday they attend, they will never be back.

When churches believe the "Christian Myths" about visitors, they have the misconception, "Well, if they want to come back and be a part of this church, they'll come back on their own." I had one pastor tell me that if visitors came back two or three times, then he would reach out to them. My only question to that pastor was, "What is going to make them want to come back?" He did not have the answer to that question. (It was obvious, since more than 90 percent of his visitors *never returned!*)

When we view "first-time attenders" with God's vision, then even the act of going to church becomes a spiritual adventure! "First-time attenders" will be walking miracles waiting to happen, and the process of building quality relationships with them will become one of the most rewarding parts of our ministry!

The Sevenfold Vision of the Visitor

1. *God calls them "My flock."* God "owns" every visitor who walks through your church doors. He calls them "scattered sheep." They are His flock. The goal of ministry to the visitor is to bring him to a place of "ownership" of your church. That means he is willing to invest his time and money in the

church just like you do. The visitor will not "own" the church unless we first "own" him. He will only become part of us if we first relate to him as though he is already part of us. You estrange visitors when you treat them like strangers. You first "own" the visitor, then the visitor will "own" you.

2. *Visitors are miracles disguised as needs.* A miracle is when the need (the visitor) meets the solution (the Care minister). God can't do a miracle without a need. God won't do a miracle without a believer to minister it. Visitors attend your church with one question: "Can you meet my needs?" The church that meets the needs of the visitors will grow.

3. *Visitors are divine appointments.* The devil never gets anybody to go to church—God does. It is not by accident that first-time attenders are there; it's by appointment.

4. *Visitors are not visitors; they are the best friends you have been looking for.* If you are lonely, lead someone to the Lord, and he will be your best friend for the rest of his life. When you minister to someone through the power and love of the Spirit of God, he becomes indebted to you because you met his need! Friends are the result of ministry.

5. *Visitors are the future church.* Too many church folk make a big difference between church members and visitors, as if the church members are special and important and visitors are *not!* At one time we were all visitors, and not members.

6. *Visitors are not visitors; they are "first-time attenders."* The only difference between a visitor and a member is this is the first (not the last) Sunday for the visitor.

7. *Visitors are not visitors; visitors are ripe fruit.* The most receptive people to the ministry God has placed in you are the people we mistakenly call "visitors."

Visitors don't come to your church to meet the needs of the church; they come expecting the church to meet their needs! How are you going to meet these needs? It won't happen from the pulpit, but from personal ministry. Where hurting people are concerned, personal ministry as a friend is more powerful than pulpit ministry.

Five Ways to Be a Friend

1. Spend time in fellowship with visitors in church. (Some people are very shy, and they feel awkward about starting conversations. If you would like help in this area, I recommend our *Care Ministry Team Member Manual.* It contains pages of questions and dialogue to help you begin conversations, discover needs, and minister to new friends

with ease. See the back of this book for a phone number to call.)

2. Ask them: "Is there anything I can pray about with you?" You should have that question memorized. It is "a miracle-working question."

3. Suggest more fellowship: "Hey, let's get together this week." Make an appointment for a specific date, time, and place.

4. Invite the first-time attenders back to church. Let them know their presence and personal happiness are important to you.

5. Go on a "cookie crusade"! Drop by their house with a gift of cookies during the week.

Three Negatives of Ignoring the Harvest

When we fail to minister to the harvest God brings in, we are ignoring God's strategy; therefore, we will reap three unwelcome results, according to the "parable of the sower" Jesus shared with His disciples (see Mt. 13:1-23). In a way, the people God brings through the church door are like seed being given to the Church. He holds us accountable for how we "steward" His precious seed.

1. *The birds eat the seed* (and therefore, the harvest). Satan's emissaries devour any seed that isn't planted and covered. Visitors who walk into

the church and walk back out *after we fail to minister to them* will be prime targets for satanic attack. The enemy will be waiting to harass visitors outside the door (if they are not already being oppressed inside the doors). He will be quick to drop little nuggets of bitterness into their minds to "help them" express their pain: "These people don't love me; they don't care about me. I guess God doesn't love me or care about me either! I don't even think God knows I exist. I don't even know why I came to church. Nobody is paying attention to me—besides, nothing here is relevant to the problems in my life. This church business is nothing!" The seed of a miracle has just been devoured through neglect.

2. *Someone else will gather the harvest.* Neglected visitors will limp out of your church with their needs unmet, saying, "This is the worst church I've ever been to—it's horrible! Nobody cares about me here. I'm going to find a church that cares about me!" If they do attend another church, their negative experience at yours makes them less receptive. God had sent the "first-time attenders" through the door for a divine appointment, but nobody from the church "showed up." Since this church wasn't willing to keep its divine appointments, God had to send His "ripe

fruit" to someone who cared. This was a missed opportunity through neglect.

3. *The harvest rots on the ground.* This is perhaps the most sickening scenario of the three! When God sends precious seeds of the miraculous through our doors, we receive it, but through neglect we allow it to just fall to the ground and rot! Every week, hurting people enter our churches with hope that they will find evidence of a real God and real love inside our doors. They quickly become disillusioned with the insensitive and uncaring church people, and decide to stay home on Sundays and watch TV instead. This is where the thousands of disillusioned and unchurched masses are found in America today, because the Church has failed to *meet the needs of people*!

We must see to the needs of every first-time attender who comes near us. We need to overcome our own myths and misconceptions and see the vision of the visitor through God's eyes. We need to feel their pain as if it were our own! People need more than sermons—they are desperately in need of *personal* care, *personal* ministry, and *personal* involvement!

How to Be Moved by Compassion

When you are moved by compassion, you will not miss your divine appointment. Passion will rearrange your priorities. Passion will position you to discover the miracles in church every week! Passion will mobilize the "last days army of God" to gather in the harvest and change people's lives by the power of the Spirit! Now how are you going to be moved by compassion? Take these three steps to release the compassion of God in your life:

1. *Repent.* Compassion is not natural. Being selfish is natural.

2. *Pray about the "Seven Conditions of Hurting Sheep"* every Sunday before you get to church. You will be giving the Spirit "ammunition" to bring these conditions to your remembrance so you can discern needs more effectively. Go to church prepared for ministry.

3. *Practice.* Every time your church meets, go around shaking hands, and try to sense what the Holy Spirit is telling you about people. Ask each of them, "Is there anything I can pray about with you?" Church members can be lonely, discouraged, and oppressed too! They can also feel condemned and hungry, and they may be hurt and wounded as well. Practice on people. The only way you'll get better at the Care Ministry is by doing it.

This Sunday, you can be a miracle. This Sunday, you can find someone who needs the Lord, who needs the love and faith that is in your heart. You are a "miracle waiting to happen," and now you know the needs that are waiting for you.

Endnote

1. *Merriam Webster's Collegiate Dictionary*, 10th Edition (Springfield, MA: Merriam-Webster, Inc., 1994), p. 234.

Chapter 4

How to Be a Miracle

Dean Roberts' first experience as a member of one of our first Care Teams dramatically illustrates what it means to "be a miracle." This is the story of his encounter with a man named Sam:

I began working in the Care Ministry because I had a desire to see people saved, but I had never had much success trying to evangelize on my own. One Sunday morning I was at the back of the auditorium, simply being available as the pastor concluded his message. A young man about my age responded and quietly went forward. I gulped and went to the front and stood beside him as the pastor led him in a prayer of confession, forgiveness, and salvation in Christ.

When I introduced myself to Sam and briefly reviewed the plan of salvation with him, the tears in his eyes told me this was for real. I made an appointment to visit him at his home, and as we left, we met Sam's wife, Sheri. God had answered her diligent prayers that morning. I knew I had witnessed a miracle because I had been available to God.

Three days later, I talked with Sheri in her dining room. She had lots of questions, but by the time Sam came in, Sheri knew I had no ulterior motives. Sam and I reviewed the salvation plan again, and I found that he had been reading the Bible and had lots of questions. The Holy Spirit helped me answer them, and I encouraged him to keep reading. After we talked about baptism, Sam wanted to be baptized on Sunday. Sam was excited and Sheri could see a genuine change in her husband.

God began to build a love in my heart for this couple. Sam was baptized on Sunday, and on Tuesday evening we met again at the dining room table. We met several more times in the following weeks, and Sam often called me with questions about the Scriptures.

I introduced Sam and Sheri to some of our Christian friends, and we formed a small home group motivated by the desire to help Sam grow. We built the group meetings around our Care Ministry team, and began to bear one another's burdens and support each other. Sam grew and became a part as we reached out to give our love and caring to visitors we met at church.

We brought visitors along with us to each group meeting and many were touched by God. We always prayed for the first-time attenders and for any other pressing needs. The first time Sam prayed for one of our guests, he poured out God's compassion from the depths of his heart, and tears flowed from his eyes. I watched in awe, knowing God had changed a cold-hearted, uncaring, self-centered, and aloof man into a compassionate minister who cared for the needs of others!

More than once he brought the people he met on Sunday to our group meetings. His work life changed, his relationship with his wife changed, and he continued diligently in the Scriptures. He wanted others to know God and experience the good things He had for them.

Sam had entered into God's Kingdom thinking "normal Christianity" consisted of meeting others' needs, seeing people get saved and baptized, and living a vital Christian life within the church. He had seen, but not tasted, stagnancy, barrenness, and loneliness in the lives of other Christians, but he was approaching his life in Christ the right way—*he was learning how to be a miracle!*

Are You an Impact Player?

Do you know who Joe Montana is? Even the ladies seem to know who Joe Montana is (not because he is arguably the greatest quarterback in history, but because he's good-looking). I watched Joe play for the Kansas City Chiefs for two years, and I noticed that Joe is an *impact player.* When Joe is on the field, the offensive line is better and the running backs run better. When he shows up, the defensive team defends better and the announcers even seem to announce better! Everything is better when Joe is on the field. Why? *He is an impact player.*

An impact player makes everyone around him better. He is not controlled by circumstances or overcome by difficulties. He has the confidence and faith to believe he can change the circumstances and win! *God saved you to be an impact player!* When you go to church, the church service will be better because you showed up in all of the anointing God has endowed in you. Would you like to be an impact player for God?

To be everything God wants you to be, you must become skilled in the two impact dynamics that are yours as a believer: *the power of the Spirit of God,* and *the power of the love of God.* If you want to be an impact player, you must focus on developing the "Three Skills of the Spirit." These include what I call "the habit of His presence," "faith to unlock the adventure," and "availability for miracles."

The Habit of His Presence

"But his delight is in the law of the Lord, and in His law [Word] he meditates day and night" (Ps. 1:2). An impact player has productive preparation habits. He puts the Word of faith in his spirit every day so he can be productive, withstand adversity, and prosper in whatever he does. Your habits will either keep you in the adventure of the Spirit or keep you trapped in the bondage of the flesh. Your habits determine your character, and your character determines your destiny!

The adventure of the Spirit is simply being the best that God created and saved you to be. Many believers miss God's best, not because they are not gifted or spiritual, but because they have not developed the right habits to achieve the greatness God has for them. Good habits are developed through practice and patience.

How to Establish Impact Player Habits:

1. *Establish a time.* Make an appointment with God. This is the most important appointment of the day because you are meeting the most important Person you know—God! He will empower and tell you secrets about the day, so this is an appointment you cannot afford to miss.

2. *Establish a place.* Meet with God in a place where there are no distractions. Don't meet Him where you do all your work; then your thoughts will turn to work and not to God. You may have to meet with God after the kids are in bed or at school.

3. *Establish an agenda.* Know what you are going to read and what you will pray about, but let God interrupt your agenda as He chooses. This gives

Him an opportunity to speak to you. God communicates more through daily experiences than through "burning bushes."

4. *Keep a journal.* Write down what you talked about with the Lord, and record what you sensed He said to you. Keep a record of every prayer that is answered. (Tip: The best time to journal is in the evening.)

Faith to Unlock the Adventure

The righteous must live by faith, and it takes *faith* to "unlock the adventure" of God's best each day. The second "Skill of the Spirit" involves three keys to unlock the power of faith in your daily life.

1. *Praise Him—it is the doorway to the adventure of God.* The Psalmist wrote, "Enter His gates with thanksgiving, and His courts with praise..." (Ps. 100:4). Praise releases your faith by setting your focus on God the Miracle-Worker instead of on yourself. The adventure of the Spirit is discovering God's will and enjoying all He has for you.

2. *Pray in the Spirit.* The Bible tells us to build up our faith by praying in the Spirit (see Jude 20). Visitors will contact God through your life *if you are in contact with God!* God has ordained "divine appointments" for every day and every church service. You must "walk in the Spirit" to know where and how to make your appointments.

3. *Confess your faith.* You will either speak your faith or speak your doubts. What you speak before church will determine your ministry when you get there. God's Word is the *sword* of the Spirit. It is a powerful offensive weapon in the spiritual realm, so use it properly to strengthen your faith and pull down strongholds (see 2 Cor. 10:4-5 KJV).

Be Available for a Miracle

The third "Skill of the Spirit" involves obedience-of-faith acts. God will work a miracle through you if you give Him the opportunity by making yourself available. *Availability is the doorway into the adventure of supernatural ministry in the Spirit!* The first step to making yourself available is to change your attitude: *"Attitude determines altitude."* Your attitude about yourself and your life determines how high you will go in God! God is a great God, and He wants you to demonstrate it by living a life of greatness! Adjust your attitude for maximum altitude so you can step into your "supernatural adventure"!

Five Steps Into Adventure

As you take the five steps leading to the adventure of supernatural ministry of the Spirit each day, you will experience divine intervention, divine appointments, and the abundance of God's grace. Each step will change your attitudes even more and lift you up to the altitude of miracles. You face a choice every day: "Do I want to live a mediocre life today, or do I dare to live a life of greatness?"

Step 1: *Get up for the adventure.* See the end from the beginning. You are not simply getting up to go to Sunday service. You are getting up to enter the adventure of the Spirit as an agent of the Almighty! To walk in the altitude of miracles, you must get up in time to prepare for the adventure!

Step 2: *Pray up into the adventure.* Prayer changes the spiritual realm. Prayer is the primary weapon that empowers you to change the spiritual realm. The spiritual realm is the realm of *cause*, and the natural realm is the realm of *effect*. Changes in the spirit realm *always* bring changes in the natural realm. You make things happen when you pray. When you enter into the spiritual realm in prayer, you can discern things in the Spirit about the divine appointments for that day! God has made you to be an "impact player" in the most significant realm of creation: the spiritual realm.

Step 3: *Build up your faith for the adventure.* Faith is the "switch that turns on the power of God." If you want to release the power of the Spirit, you must know how to use the skill of faith.

Step 4: *Look up for the adventure.* If you expect nothing, nothing will happen; but if you expect a miracle, you may find a miracle! Most Christians don't experience the "adventure of the Spirit" because they expect God to move through the pastor, not them! The needs in any service or church body are greater than the pastor can manage. That is why God has saved you to work miracles. When you "look up," *you are looking for a need.* God can't do a miracle without a need. Remember, visitors are not visitors; visitors are miracles disguised as a need. A need is simply the beginning of a miracle!

Step 5: *Step up into the adventure.* Boldness releases the anointing. Once you see a need, do something about it. Step up to the person and begin to relate with him, so you can earn the right to minister to his need. God will never do a miracle through you if you don't give Him an opportunity. When you are willing to pray for someone with a need, it is miracle time!

The Impact Dynamic of God's Love

At the beginning of this chapter, we learned that to be an impact player for God, we must become skilled in the two impact dynamics that are ours as believers: the power of the Spirit of God, and the power of the love of God. The impact dynamic of God's love involves three critical sets of skills. *Your skill level and abilities in all three areas will directly affect every area of your life!*

You can impact people just as effectively with the love of God as you can the power of God. However, to impact people *relationally*, you must know how to effectively use the "skills of love." I use the word *skills* because these areas involve training, and they have very little to do with your personality, temperament, or past experience. The skills of love involve learning how to communicate and respond to people, and they are learned through practice. I have been practicing these skills for years, and I continue to practice them every day.

Love Is a Bridge

We have to build a "bridge of love" if we want to change people's lives. That "bridge" of love will transport the truth within us into the hearts of others. Without this bridge, the hurting will not hear the truth. Love demonstrated becomes a bridge of trust. It is the only way to "earn the right" to speak into people's lives. You cannot just go up to somebody and expect him to give you his life—it won't happen. There are proven ways to build a bridge of love so you can effectively communicate God's love to others. The skills of love include the areas of relational skills, communicational skills, and interview skills. These skills are useful in every area of life.

1. *Relational skills* allow you to encourage people to trust you and like you. You can't "make" anyone trust you, but you can "invite" people to like you and trust you.

2. *Communication skills* help you to encourage people to share their needs with you. The Care Ministry is a "need-fulfillment ministry," but you will not know what needs to meet if you do not know how to *discover* a person's needs. The key to success as a Care minister is to find a need and fill it, to find a hurt and heal it.

3. *Interview skills* help you invite people to share their lives with you. They help you to become their friend, and to discover what is important to them.

Relational Skills: Three Attitudes of the Heart

There are three attitudes of the heart that govern all our ministry and our efforts to relate to others. When the heart is right, we will still manage to meet the needs of others even when we do the wrong things through ignorance or lack of training!

1. *The Attitude of Love*

Your attitude of love is expressed through the main goal of Care Team Ministry: to meet needs. An attitude of love says, "I want to meet your need." The Care Ministry is a need-fulfillment ministry, not merely a "church growth ministry" trying to get visitors to become members! We have the same goal Jesus had: We want to meet the needs of the people God brings to us! We want visitors to encounter the heart of God. We want them to experience His care for them, His mercy to meet their needs, and His power to release them from the oppression of the evil one. Again, we believe that the key to our success is to "find a need and fill it, find a hurt and heal it."

2. *The Attitude of Confidence*

Your attitude of confidence says, "You are going to like me. We are going to be good friends." Your best friend will be the person you lead to the Lord. Think about the person who led you to the Lord. Didn't you think he was wonderful? Didn't you want to be that individual's friend? To minister effectively to people you must believe people will like you before they meet you. You must understand this relational principle: People's opinions of you come primarily from one source—your opinion of yourself. You determine what people think about you more than anyone else.

Have you ever been around a nervous salesman? You didn't know why he was nervous, but he made you nervous too, didn't he? If you want to minister to people, you cannot be worried about what they think about you. Still you think, *I wonder if they will like me?*

When you approach someone, your attitude of confidence is, "Hi, my name is Ken Houts, and you are going to like me!" If you think that is strange, think about the alternative: "Hi, my name is Ken Houts, you're not going to like me, and I don't know why I am talking to you!" But the big question in so many believers' minds is, "How can I think that about myself? After all, how do I know that someone is going to like me?" The problem is in your thinking. You don't see yourself the way God sees you. Many believers see themselves the way the devil sees them and not the way God sees them. God does not see you defined by the past, but defined by your destiny—the way He made you to be.

Which picture of you is more accurate: yours or God's? Let's find out God's picture of you from the Bible. "I will give thanks to Thee, for I am fearfully and wonderfully made; wonderful are Thy works, *and my soul knows it very well*" (Ps. 139:14).

The last phrase defines the verse. I understand that creationists use this verse to say King David was thanking God for his physiological creation. Although that has application, I believe David woke up one morning, lifted his hands to the Lord, and said, "God, I thank You that You made me wonderful. Wonderful are Thy works." David saw himself as a wonderful person— spirit, soul, and body. Everything God made about him, God made wonderful. David was a wonderful person. David's soul also knew it "very well." He did not have feelings of insecurity or inferiority because his soul knew he was wonderful. Why? God made him that way!

Now if God made King David wonderful, did He make you wonderful too? Or did the Lord say, "Oops" when He made you? God didn't say "Oops," the Lord said, "You are wonderful!" when He made you! The difference between David and so many believers today is that David knew he was wonderful. His soul knew it deep inside, while many believers still struggle with knowing they are what God made them.

Confidence begins with agreeing with what God's Word says about you. The Word of God says you are wonderful, so you are wonderful. Every wonderful person I know is also likable and lovable. Since the Lord made you wonderful, He also made you likable and lovable. God made you a wonderful, lovable, likable person.

Just the way you are, right now, people will like you. That is the way God made you. Confidence is the result of believing how the Lord made you: wonderful, lovable, and likable!

3. *The Attitude of Acceptance*

Visitors must feel accepted by us just the way they are as well. If we do not accept them because they talk differently, dress differently, or act differently, they will feel like we are looking down on them, and they will never come back. We will not be able to minister to them or lead them to the Lord if they never come back for more ministry.

What is the best way to communicate acceptance? You smile! Smiles communicate warmth, acceptance, and safety. When you smile you say, "I accept you, I like you, and I'm safe." Smiles disarm distrust, and invite people to trust you. The most important relational skill you practice every day of your life is to smile. I watched Robert Schuller on TV when he told the story about a woman who was channel surfing until she came upon Brother Schuller's smile. When he said, "God loves you, and so do I!" she was captivated by the warmth and love of his smile. She watched the entire program and came to the Lord. She got saved from his smile. Never underestimate the power of your smile.

When you approach visitors in church to talk to them, before you even reach them, make eye contact and smile at them. You want your first contact with them to be your smile. Do you know what they will think when they see you smiling at them? "Here comes a wonderful, lovable, likable kind of guy! I'm going to like him!" The first experience visitors will have with you is your smile. Smile during the conversation; communicate that you are enjoying talking to them. Finally, their last picture of you as you say good-bye is you smiling. What would happen if everyone in church smiled? If everyone that the guests talked to smiled at them? Visitors would think yours was the happiest church in town. When you smile you become an enjoyable person to be around, and the joy of the Lord is released in your smile.

Three Ways to Make the Visitor Feel Important

Do you enjoy being with people who make you feel unimportant? What do you do with those people? You stay away from them, don't you? Do you know how visitors feel in most churches? Unimportant. Why? They *are* unimportant to most good church folk. The important people in church are not the visitors. After all, they are only "visitors" and they probably won't be around next week anyway. Who are the important people in church? First, the pastor is the most important person in church, and we treat him that way. Then there is the board, the staff, the choir, the teachers, etc. Finally way down the list of important people you want to talk to are the visitors. So they feel unimportant to the church.

If the church does not intentionally make visitors feel important, we will unintentionally make them feel unimportant. If you communicate to visitors that they are important to you, then you will become important to them.

Remember the Most Important Word

The most important word in a person's life is his name. The sweetest sound to anyone's ears is his name. You can relate with people in many ways to make them feel important, but none of that matters if you do not repeat their name. When you remember the name of someone and repeat it, you have told them, "You are important to me, because your name is important to me." There are three ways to remember a person's name. First, write it down. Most times your memory is no longer than your pen. Since you now attend church to minister, come prepared with a pen and pad. Ask Frank Visitor his name, then say, "Frank, I have a horrible time with names. Would it be all right if I wrote your name down?" Another method is to repeat the visitor's name at least 5 or 6 times. The simple way to do this is to begin or end the sentence with his name. Remember, you cannot say someone's name too many times. Finally, there is word association. Be careful! I heard of a salesman who was attempting to remember a client's name, Mrs. Snodgrass. He was using word association to remember her name. But then in a phone call he said, "Hello, Mrs. Boogernose..."!

Care for the Most Important People

Children are the most important people to their parents. Always make friends with the children. Once I have met the parents, I immediately introduce myself to the children. I love to have fun with children, so if they do not shake my extended hand, I tickle them to make them laugh. I want children to know I genuinely care for them. You become important to the parents when you make their children important to you.

Give Attention to Make People Feel Important

Do you remember being with someone you thought was very important to you? It may have been a president of a large corporation, or some person of accomplishment. Do you remember how you listened to him, and hung on every word? You made that person feel important by the attention you gave him. Attention is a rare commodity in our society today. Everyone wants it, but few give it. In ministry, our goal is for all whom we talk with to feel like they are the president of a large company. When visitors feel important to you, they will want to be with you. Giving visitors attention enables you to earn the right to minister to their needs.

In order to impact someone with this type of attention, you first make this relational decision when you begin talking to him: *"This person is the most important person to me in the whole world."* When you make that decision, then what they say is important to you, not because of its content, nor because you relate to it, but because the person is important to you. When you talk with visitors on Sunday, your goal of love is for them to feel heard, understood, accepted, and appreciated. You must listen to the mundane to discover the pain. Ministry begins by giving the attention people need to feel important enough to you. Then they will share their needs with you.

Once you make that decision, then follow these three steps to invite guests to share their lives and needs with you. First, *be totally there for them.* Do not interrupt your conversation with them to speak to someone else. Be totally there with them as long as the conversation lasts. Second, *make eye contact.* Eye contact is the most powerful means of giving attention and encouraging someone to talk. Third, ask *"What" and "how" opened-ended questions.* These encourage people to talk, which is what they want to do.

Communication Skills: Tap the Power of Two-Way Communication

We share our lives with other people through two primary communication skills: listening and speaking. *Listening is the secret of communication.* After all, which skill is more important for you to be a good communicator: listening or speaking? Seventy-five percent of all communication is listening! You will not know what to say to another person until you have heard what he has said. The art and skill of listening equips you for ministry in four very important ways.

1. *Listening equips you to understand.* You have nothing to say until you have heard the needs, wants, and problems of the other person. Your communication will be ineffective if you fail to *listen first!* The worst thing you can do in communication is to close someone out while he is still talking so you can "think of what you're going to say" to him in return!

I was seated on a crowded commuter plane one time when an older gentleman asked me if I would consider changing seats with his associate. I thought about it, but since my large frame could barely fit in the aisle seat as it was, I politely refused. The older gentleman smiled and took his seat next to me anyway, and began the normal traveling conversation about "what we do." When religion came up, he suddenly cut off the conversation. But at one point, he said he had been retired for more than 30 years, so I asked him, "What made you so successful that you could retire thirty years ago?" That one question began a one-sided conversation that lasted the rest of the flight.

He talked and I actively listened. Just before we landed, he said, "Ken, I like you. I don't know why I like you, but I do." He then said, "I want you to play golf with me the next time you are in California." He was a millionaire who lived on a golf course, and he gave me his name, address, and phone number. When was the last time you had a millionaire give you his address and phone number to play golf? Why did he like me so much? He liked me because I cared about him, and I made him feel important. I did it by listening to him!

2. *Listening equips you with compassion.* Compassion is feeling what another person is feeling. This puts you in the same place as our compassionate God, who feels our pain. Compassion lets you know how to respond to a person's pain. You must learn to listen with your heart, not just your

ears. This lets you hear more than mere words. You will hear another's soul.

3. *Listening equips you with bonding by the Spirit.* The most effective ministry takes place in relationships that have been *bonded by the Spirit of God.* When the bonding occurs, trust grows, openness occurs, and friendships are born. Each of those crucial elements of relationship hinge on your ability to listen!

4. *Listening creates divine appointments.* In recent years, I was invited to conduct a workshop on the Care Ministry for the regional convention of a large denomination of churches. I knew that the newly selected leader of the national organization was scheduled to speak at the same convention, and realized that it would obviously be advantageous to make contact with him. I asked God for a divine appointment and if I did get an opportunity to meet with him, the Lord gave me a series of questions to help me discover the needs he was facing as the leader of 11,000 churches.

I was having lunch with some of the other workshop speakers when a personal friend of mine told me he would have to leave the luncheon early. *He had to pick up the head of this denomination at the airport!* I had prayed for a divine appointment (not a "promotional moment") that morning. I knew this was no accident, so I asked him if he would like me to go to the airport with him, and he agreed.

At the airport, the leader of the denomination gave my friend a big hug. I guess he thought I was part of the welcoming committee too, so even though we had never met, he also gave me a very warm and loving hug! On the way back to the convention site, my friend suddenly realized he had to return to the airport to pick up the pilot. He asked me, "Ken, would you take Brother So and So to the room?" I told him I would love to. I only had one problem—I didn't know where the room was located in that very large complex. When we arrived, the brother visited a rest room and I quickly found out where the main meeting hall was located. The leader returned and put his hand on my shoulder, and I led the way to the meeting!

God arranged things so that I somehow walked into the main meeting with the national leader and most influential person of the denomination. All the pastors there thought I was with him, and he thought I was with them. All I knew was that I was just glad to be there. No one knew me from Adam until I walked into the room with their national leader. Then it hit me: God just introduced me to the entire regional organization.

When the company contracted to record all the sessions forgot to equip the room where the denominational leader was speaking, I quietly told him I would take care of the problem. I knew only one person there, but that one person was the one who could solve the problem. I found him, and we quickly had the sound system functioning for the national leader's address to all the pastors. I sat in the front row next to the regional director over those pastors, and continued to *serve* the national leader.

After the meeting, I asked the leader if we could spend some time together during the next two days. He smiled and told me that "right then" would be a good time! For the next 30 minutes, we talked privately in the senior pastor's office at the host church. I began the conversation by making the only statement I would make about me or my ministry in the entire interview. I said, "Brother, I travel a lot, and I talk to a lot of pastors. *What are the problems that concern you in the fellowship?*" For the next 30 minutes, *he talked and I listened.*

We were bonded together by the Spirit because I listened with compassion. I felt his desire to see the fellowship of churches grow. I felt the urgent need he sensed for a fresh move of the Spirit among the churches, and I felt his need to help the pastors.

The next day, I happened to arrive in the parking lot at the same time as my friend, the national leader, who arrived with a car full of pastors. As I gathered my workshop material in my arms, he left the group of pastors to come over to me, put his arm around me, and walk with me into the church like an old friend. Why were we so close? Did I impress him with how great the Care Ministry is? No. I listened to his heart with pure motives and genuine concern. That gave the Holy Spirit an opportunity to bond us together.

After the convention, this man agreed to let me visit him at his office at the national denominational headquarters. I carefully spelled out the reason for my visit in a letter, and included some promotional material and a video about the Care Ministry. When I arrived, we talked briefly, and I noticed that he had my material on his desk. When I asked him if he'd had an opportunity to view the video, he said he hadn't. Then he caught me by surprise when he said, "Ken, I want you to speak at our General Convention next year." I was shocked! I had not told him anything about the Care Ministry and he had not viewed my video, so he did not know what the Care Ministry would do for the fellowship of churches. Yet he had asked me to speak at the General Conference for all the denomination's churches in the nation! Why? I gave the Holy Spirit an opportunity to bond us together when I laid aside my own agenda and took the time to listen to this man of God.

Two months later, I heard this man say during a sermon, "I don't do anything without praying and hearing God, because that is the only way to know that you are doing the right thing." Right then I heard God say, "Ken, I arranged the divine appointment, and I want you to speak at the General Convention." This was divine-human cooperation. God opened the door, and I walked in by faith. I listened, and God confirmed it.

Listening will equip you to open doors that nothing else will, because *listening gets God involved!* The Care Ministry is 80 percent listening and 20 percent talking. The Care Ministry is a successful need-fulfillment ministry because it is dedicated to the key principle of success: "Find a need and fill it, find a hurt and heal it."

Speaking is the second key element of communication. There are three components that communicate when we speak. Which of the three components is the most important?

1. Body language.

2. Tone of voice.

3. Words.

Which of the three has the greatest impact on people when we talk to them? Research has yielded some surprising facts about the way these elements impact listeners:

- 38 percent of all communication is tone of voice.

- 55 percent of all communication is body language.

- 7 percent of all communication is the words that we use.

People often tell me, "Ken, I want to be in the Care Ministry, but I don't know what to say." The fact is that it doesn't matter! If you love and care for people enough to listen to them, then you will communicate *the right thing* even when you say the wrong thing! People won't walk out of church and say, "Boy, do you remember what they said to me?" No, they walk out of church thinking, "Boy, those people really love us." That is exactly what we want them to remember!

The Five Levels of Communication

The deeper you go into communication, the closer you will get to hearing the real need in a person's life. Communication involves at least five levels: cliché, facts, opinion, emotions and feelings, and "peak experience."

Communication on the "cliché level" consists of light remarks like, "Hi. How are you doing?" Religious clichés include phrases like, "Praise the Lord. Hallelujah! You're good, I'm fine. Hallelujah, I've got the victory, you've got the victory, we all got the victory. I'm blessed, you're blessed. Hallelujah!" The cliché is appropriate in the grocery store aisle when we pass people and say, "Hi. How are you doing?" We just hope they won't say, "My dog died, my garage door fell off, my dishwasher fell apart, and my husband left me last night." We don't want that information—we want them to say, "I'm fine." Cliché is good, but ministry only takes place when we get beyond the cliché.

Communication on the "fact level" majors on factual questions and answers, such as, "Where do you live? How long have you lived there?" This obviously has a place, but it will never help us discover the pain in a person's life.

The communication of opinion is our first real window into the heart and needs of a person. Everyone loves to tell people what he thinks. The more we understand people, the more we can meet their needs.

The communication of emotions and feelings reveals the "fingerprint" of the soul. We may "think" the same thing about something, but we will all have different "feelings" about it. When you get to the feeling level, *you begin to touch the pain.* When someone shares an experience, either good or bad, ask: "How do you feel about it?" Only by understanding the emotional level of response will you truly be able to serve others.

The fifth level of communication is "peak experience." People are communicating at the "peak" when two people feel heard, understood, accepted, and loved because of communication! Husbands and wives desperately need peak experiences. They feel fulfilled and satisfied when they feel that they are heard and understood.

When you begin communicating with someone, you need to have an idea of where you are going with the conversation. These five levels are *indications of where you want to go.* Start with the cliché, move on to facts about events and experiences, and then ask for an opinion about the event. But don't stop there. When you discover how someone feels, you will discover his pain and how you can help and bless him.

Interview Skills: The Search for Relationship

Interview skills effectively increase your ability to invite people to share their lives and needs with you. You will need these interview skills to effectively meet the needs of the first-time attenders.

The A.I.D. Communication System

This simple system of communication helps to begin a conversation, keep it on track until you are able to discover a person's needs, and puts you in a "relational position" to meet the needs. "A.I.D." stands for *Approach*, *Interview*, and *Demonstration*.

The *Approach* step reminds you it is time to become a visitor's friend. People generally do not share their pain with strangers. This is a time to ask visitors questions about what is important to them. Learn about their spouse, their children, their hobbies, and even their sports interests.

The *Interview* step is a time of discovery and need development. If you are going to meet people's needs, you must understand their needs. This is a crucial step, because if they do not have needs, then you have nothing to give them except unconditional love. Need development is simply having others agree they have a need for the Lord to intervene in their lives. This makes it much easier for you to pray for their specific needs.

The *Demonstration* stage is the point at which we demonstrate our love for visitors and put action to our desire to meet their need. Our first expression of the love of God is to pray for them and release the power of God in their lives. It is always good to touch those you pray for, either by holding their hand, or laying your hand on their shoulder—but always *ask permission* before doing this.

The I.E.N. Principle

The I.E.N. principle is another powerful tool to help you develop better interview skills and open the doors into people's lives. "I.E.N." stands for *Interest, Entertainment,* and *Needs,* the three practical doors into people's lives.

When you interview visitors, ask about their *interests*! What interests do they have? Is it their job, their children, their family, their hobbies, sports, or their church? What issue in life brings them the most fulfillment? If you are asking yourself, "How am I going to find out what brings fulfillment to the first-time attenders at the church?" well, the solution is very simple—ask them.

Then ask them what they do for *entertainment*. We are an entertainment-driven society. Billions of dollars are spent to entertain us. Entertainment is a topic that is very interesting to them, and they will be quick to talk to someone who is interested in the same form.

Learning about any one of these areas in a visitor's life will give you an opportunity to talk to him about things that interest him. When I do not know very much about a person's interest area, I just let him educate me about what is important to him!

The most important, and most difficult, area to ask about is the area of personal *needs*. The time you invest in discussing *what is important to a visitor* will usually open up an opportunity to find out where he is hurting. This is truly "need-fulfillment ministry." Now people may not let you in the door of need initially, but they may let you in the door of interest.

Remember: You are trying to find the door into a visitor's life so you can become his friend and meet his needs! You are not wanting a working relationship, but a personal relationship. The only way we can meet first-time attenders' needs, and the only way we can bring them into the life of the church, is by *investing the time to become their friend.* If you are willing to spend just a few hours relating with someone to enter the doors of their lives, you will find yourself becoming a "door" to Jesus Christ and the church! As you practice the skills of love, you will discover that people will let you into their lives, and you will begin to experience divine appointments of the Holy Spirit.

Chapter 5

Relationships Empower You for Miracles

Alfonso was born and raised in another country where, through the influence of family members, he became involved in organized crime. His mother moved to the United States with her sons to break away from this influence, but Alfonso became involved with it again. His criminal activities caused his mother much frustration, fear, and sadness, since she never knew what trouble or what jail he might be in. At times she wondered if he would come home alive or be carried home dead. Alfonso brought shame to the family, yet he had no intention of changing. He was a curse to his mother.

While Alfonso was still a young man, God began to deal with him through a number of circumstances. Alfonso began to want to change, but still could not. Finally he cried out to God, who sent some Christian friends to help him. Alfonso was saved, and he began to build a godly life. He got a job, left his old ways behind, and got involved in church. He became a member of a Care Team led by my friend, Dean Roberts, one of the original Care Team leaders who has experienced a very successful ministry as a group leader and coordinator.

One night, Alfonso told the Care Team that his mother, who lived far away, had been diagnosed with a serious illness, and that she was afraid. Alfonso had encouraged her to trust God to heal her, and he prayed with her on the phone. He told the group that the day before the Care Team meeting, he had spoken to his mother again. He suddenly broke into tears, but then he continued to tell the story with his strong accent. He told the group that his mother had said, "There must be something wonderful about Alfonso's God, because the doctor told me I no longer have the disease!" Alfonso grinned and told us, "I love my mother, and I thank God!"

Dean Roberts, his Care Group leader, said, "By the end of Alfonso's story, many of us were fighting back tears as we rejoiced in the miracles of God. First, this was a miraculous healing in answer to prayer. Secondly, God had miraculously changed Alfonso's life. He had been transformed from a curse to a blessing right before his mother's eyes! Thirdly, this man, who was very different from us, felt very much like our brother, and we hugged him, prayed for him, and thanked God with him."

Ezekiel and Alfonso in the New Testament

Alfonso reminds me of the bones in Ezekiel's prophecy. By all rights, he shouldn't have been in that home shedding tears and worshiping God with those Care Team ministers. He had been a career criminal in his native country and here in the U.S. He was a hardened parasite preying on society, and he was as good as dead in his tortured mother's eyes. But God had His own plans for Alfonso—that young man was destined to be part of God's great end-time army of miracle workers! God saved Alfonso from ruin through loving, giving relationships with His people. This is the very heart of the Care Ministry in the church.

Ezekiel described how the army of God will be raised up from the pile of dry bones:

"And I will put sinews [ligaments] *on you, make flesh grow back on you, cover you with skin, and put breath in you that you may come alive; and you will know that I am the Lord." So I prophesied as I was commanded; and as I prophesied, there was a noise, and behold, a rattling; and the bones came together, bone to its bone* (Ezekiel 37:6-7).

Ezekiel saw a pile of bones that would become the army of God. The first act of the Spirit was to draw those bones together: "bone to its bone." God's army in our day will only rise up as the bones come together. In many churches today, dry bones meet together in a single pile, but they are not *joined* together. They are not an army coming to life; they are an army drying out in a graveyard! What will make today's church become the army of God? The apostle Paul has an answer that should change the way we look at the church!

Paul urged the Ephesian believers to grow up into Christ, the head of the Church, "from whom the whole body, being fitted and held together by that which every joint supplies, according to the proper working of each individual part, causes the growth of the body for the building up [or strengthening] of itself in love" (Eph. 4:16). You are fitted or bonded together with other "bones" in Christ's Body by "spiritual joints." These "joints" provide you with spiritual stability while you labor with the other "bones" to produce growth and new strength in the church in love.

What Is a Joint?

A physical joint is where two parts come together. I have to admit that I am not very mechanical. In fact, when I pick up a tool at home, my children begin to laugh and say, "Dad, put that thing down before you hurt yourself. Let Mom do it." However, even though I am not mechanical, I have observed certain ways the natural realm works.

I know that a "dovetail joint" describes a special way the parts of my kitchen cabinets are joined together for maximum strength without the use of nails or staples. I have learned that a "trap joint" describes the way two parts of the plumbing come together under a sink. In our physical bodies, our bones are brought together "bone to its bone" in our joints. The joints in the Body of Christ are *interpersonal relationships.*

Old Testament Prophecy Fulfilled!

Contrary to popular belief, spiritual unity is not a theological issue! We do not experience the unity of the Spirit because we mentally agree; God joins us at the heart, not the head. Unity of spirit does not come by belonging to the same association, fellowship, or denomination. Unity is not an ecclesiastical issue, but a relational issue.

The only way God's people are united is through relationships (or joints) with other people in the church. The church is more than meetings, tasks, or buildings; the church is people. You don't "go" to church—you "are" the church!

The Threefold Purpose of Relationships

Why does God unite us through relationships, and how do they affect the way we function in the church? Paul says the "joints" in the church fit us together, hold us together, and help supply spiritual needs. This is a perfect description of the "threefold purpose of relationships" in the church.

Relationships Fit Us Together

When I graduated from college, I had a degree in New Testament theology. I was educated, I could preach, I could teach, and I had gifts for the ministry, but I was not ministering because I did not fit anywhere. I heard about a church in town where a thousand young people were meeting together. I went on Sunday night, and I met the pastor after church. In that short time of fellowship, God began to bond us together. We began to have a relationship, and within three months, I was on staff and he was mentoring me in the ministry. It all began with a relationship that fit me into the ministry of the church.

Most Christians remain uninvolved and inactive in their churches because they don't feel like they fit—they don't have relationships in the church. When we don't feel like we fit or belong, we don't get involved. Relationship always precedes involvement.

1. *Relationships are the only way you belong in the church.* You do not belong to a meeting, an institution, an organization, or a corporation; you belong to people. If you do not have a sense of belonging, you will not want to invest in the church. There must first be a sense of belonging to the local church before you will invest yourself in the church. Belonging happens through relationships.

2. *Relationships are the only way you feel secure.* Ministry requires a support base, for if you make a mistake (and you will from time to time), you need someone who will support you instead of criticizing you. If you do not have relationships that support your ministry attempts, you will not take the risk to minister. There is too much to lose. Most people would rather have superficial acceptance in church than authentic rejection because they did something wrong. Eighty percent of all church members today are not functioning in the church because they "do not know anyone" in their local church! They attend church "out of joint." They are not bonded, so they do not have the security to minister.

3. *Relationships are the only way you have friends.* Church is a very lonely place when you don't have friends to support you. When you come Sunday morning, you sit by yourself and wonder if anyone really cares if you are there. It is painful to attend a meeting without belonging. We all need the support of friends to function at our best. We need their love, their support, their care, and their prayers.

4. *Relationships are the only way you feel needed.* Meetings don't need you; institutions don't need you. People need you. To really feel a part of the local church is to feel like you are needed by the people

That means you would be missed. Your gifts, your strengths, and your talents are part of the success of the ministry.

5. *Relationships are the first motivation for ministry.* The Bible calls service and ministry a "labour of love" (Heb. 6:10 KJV). Love is the first motivation for our involvement in ministry to others. Churches often require commitment from people before the church demonstrates its commitment of love toward the people, and then they complain about the poor response

Team Ministry and Relationships

Jesus did not train the disciples by starting a Bible college. He *related* to His disciples. Within that relationship, He imparted the anointing of the Spirit and released them to minister to the needs of others (see Lk. 10:1). I have seen this in my ministry through the years. Darrell Massier began to attend the church I was pastoring, took some ministry training classes there, and followed me around as I ministered to people.

He watched me lead people to the Lord, and when I went on staff at the church with 4,000 members, Darrell and his wife came with me. He was the first person I asked to be part of the Care Ministry after God revealed it to me. In the five years Darrell was involved in the Care Ministry there, he led 500 people to the Lord. His care team has also led several hundred to the Lord.

He reproduced himself in about eight or ten leaders in the church, and his group multiplied every year!

Did this just happen? This ministry was the fruit of our relationship. If you want to see a release of ministry, find someone who is doing the ministry and stay with him. You will see an increase in your own ministry. It is a biblical and spiritual reality.

Relationships Hold Us on the Ministry Team

When I was pastoring a church, I quickly discovered that I did not have the emotional energy to invest in everyone in the church. The Lord led me to invest in the men who were leading our small groups. This leadership team met every week, and I had lunch with each one of them every week. Although I invested much of myself and my time in these men, the "payback" was even greater!

Aside from the fruits of their labors, I found that the love and friendship I received from my leadership team *kept me in the ministry!* We had a common vision for the church, a common passion for the Lord, and a common love for one another. They were there for me when I needed them, and I was there when they needed me. It wasn't just because I was their pastor—we were friends.

My most rewarding times as a pastor did not come through the growth of the church, the building programs, the counseling, the preaching, or the conventions. I was rewarded by the time I was able to spend with the team who loved me and stayed with me. Love held me in the ministry. Love rewarded me more than anything the ministry had to offer!

Team relationships keep us "in place" and in the ministry when we want to quit. The devil always uses discouragement to cause you to drop out of the ministry or active roles in the church. Face it: You will encounter problems, make mistakes, and suffer setbacks as long as you are breathing. As you begin to step out in the Care Ministry, satan hopes he can weaken your faith in the vision so you will quit before you experience the miracle God has for you.

You will probably not have your miracle the first month of ministry, nor the second, nor the third. In fact, it may take you five or six months before you have your first "divine appointment"! All I have to say is: "So what? If you haven't seen anyone saved for five or six years, what difference does a short wait of five or six months make?" But relationships on the team will keep you in the ministry until your miracle comes.

Relationships Supply Spiritual Strength

Connie was another faithful member of a Care Team headed by Dean Roberts. Connie's daughter, Stacey, was an occasional church attender, and her husband, Larry, was unsaved. Stacey came to the Care Group cautiously at first, but as they began to labor with her in prayer for her husband, she opened up and became friendly with the group. The Care Group shared her joy when they saw Larry come to church with Stacey the Sunday he made Jesus the Lord of his life.

Dean told me, "I can still remember the look on Larry's face when he first visited our Care Group and discovered that he had an immediate cluster of over a dozen friends who all felt they knew him!" Another couple in the group became close friends with Larry and Stacey and helped them grow in Jesus. They even went out together regularly and took vacations together. The group also began to pray that God would bless Stacey and Larry with a child, since they were childless. The whole Care Group rejoiced the day God answered their prayers when Stacey and Larry adopted a precious baby girl!

God never intended you to walk the Christian walk by yourself. You were saved to be part of Christ's Body, to function in His army, and to belong to His family!

"God, Where Are You?"

Fred Kropp, one of the best facilitators of the Care Ministry International Team, suffered a heart attack during his years of pastoring. A heart attack is a scary and lonely experience. Fred desperately wanted to sense the presence of God in the midst of that trial, so he began to pray, "God, where are You right now?"

During the lonely ambulance ride to the hospital, Fred continued to pray, "God, where are You?" When the ambulance arrived at the hospital, Fred was preparing himself for the emergency room ordeal. But when they opened the doors to the ambulance, 30 friends from the church suddenly surrounded the ambulance wanting to know the condition of *their friend, Fred!* Right then, God spoke to Fred and said, "Here I am—I am in My people!"

In those times when we cannot feel the presence of God, we need each other. We need each other daily. Relationships are not an option for you. Relationships are your first step if you want to be part of the army of God. You receive supernatural strength when you are bonded to others with a common vision, mission, and goals. God-ordained relationships will give you the strength, support, and motivation to help you achieve your destiny in God. One thing is sure: You will never get there by yourself. Ministry flows from relationships.

The Bonds of Relationships

"...Holding fast to the head, from whom the entire body, being supplied and held together by the joints and ligaments [bonds], grows with a growth which is from God" (Col. 2:19). Just as strong ligaments hold the physical joints of our bodies together, God has ordained that *relationships* bond us together as parts of His Body, the Church. Without ligaments (relationships), we are just a pile of bones incapable of working together, growing, or handling the weight and stress of life. We would all be out of joint and useless.

Have you ever seen churches fall apart during times of stress? People leave those churches because they are not *bonded to one another in relationships*. You cannot be bonded to a church by merely attending Sunday morning church services, yet it is only the bond of relationships that empowers you to fulfill your ministry and destiny!

Without relationships bonding us together, we will not have the strength to endure adversity, disagreement, or crisis. The Bible describes two kinds of bonds or ligaments that hold our relationships together in the church: the bond of peace and the bond of love.

The Bond of Peace

Paul urged the Ephesian believers to be "...diligent to preserve the unity of the Spirit in the bond of peace" (Eph. 4:3). The source of unity in the Spirit is the peace of God. Unity of Spirit is the result of peace in our relationships. How are our relationships bonded with peace? The answer applies to every relationship we have, not just those in the church. Peace in relationships comes from trust in the heart. Trust comes when we are related to someone who is trustworthy.

Relationships without peace are dysfunctional relationships. Marriages devoid of peace are dysfunctional,

Parent-child relationships that have no peace are dysfunctional. Peace enables us to function together, and peace comes when we trust one another. Most Christians think they have peaceful relationships with almost everyone in the church because they sit in services together. The bond of peace involves much more than that.

How can we promote peace and bond together on the ministry team for the purposes of God? Peace occurs when the "relational bank account" is full. The "relational bank account" is a metaphor I use to describe the amount of trust we have built into our relationships. A "relational bank account" with a rich supply of deposits will produce feelings of safety and security in those we share it with.

You can make deposits and withdrawals in these "relational bank accounts." Just as it is with the bank on the corner, you can make more withdrawals than deposits at this "bank" and get into a whole lot of trouble. If you are "overdrawn" in a relationship, then conflict will arise.

The problem is that we don't see the problems in our relationships as "relational overdrafts." We think they come from the shortcomings in the "other person." We think that if he would just improve in his areas of weakness, then we would not be having a conflict. The only problem with that reasoning is those shortcomings were in place even when there was no relational conflict!

Have you been making withdrawals or deposits in your relationships? If you truthfully evaluate your troubled relationships, you will discover your "bank account is overdrawn"!

Examples of Relational Withdrawals:

- Criticism, faultfinding, being judgmental.

- Continually asking or demanding service from the other person.

- Taking his service for granted.

- Taking his character for granted.

- Being self-serving.

- Limiting communication.

- Exposing weaknesses to others.

- Saying one thing and doing another.

Each time you make this type of withdrawal, the emotional balance in the bank account of your relationship gets lower. If a situation arises that places demands on the relationship, you will discover you have nothing in the relationship that will motivate the person to work with you!

Examples of Relational Deposits:

- My affirmation gives you value.

- My communication gives you myself.

- My integrity gives you my word.

- My honesty gives you trust.

- My kindness gives you care.

Let me give you an example of the deposit of kindness. My wife and I celebrated our twenty-fifth wedding anniversary this year (even though everyone tells us we don't look that old). We celebrated it every day during the week. I would wake up in the morning and tell Cheryl, "Happy anniversary, honey." On Thursday, during dinner, my wife and oldest daughter Joanna decided they would go to the mall after dinner.

I said, "Ya'll go on to the mall, and I'll clean up the kitchen." After my wife picked herself up off the floor from the shock of my offer, she told me it was a great idea, and they left.

Now a wife's idea of "when the kitchen is clean" is different than a husband's idea of "when the kitchen is clean." My wife had 25 years to domesticate me, so I was trained to know what her idea of a clean kitchen was. For my wife, a clean kitchen also means a clean counter. I was determined the kitchen would be clean.

I cleared the table, rinsed the dishes and placed them in the dishwasher (praise God for dishwashers), swept the floor, and cleaned that counter. I even got the tile cleaner out to clean the counter. Two hours later the kitchen was clean, so I went into my office to finish some work.

Then Cheryl came home, went into the kitchen, and saw the clean kitchen—complete with a spotless counter. Then peace came emanating from the kitchen and filled the whole house! Peace was everywhere. Cheryl peacefully came into my office to hug and kiss me. Why? I had made a deposit of caring about her. She didn't have to spend two hours in the kitchen cleaning up after coming home from shopping. Caring is a big deposit.

The Five Bonds of Love

Above all, put on love, which is the mature bond of unity (Colossians 3:14, the "Houts translation").

Unity of the Spirit is the result of bonding, not doctrine or church involvement. It flows from relationships. Love bonds us together in unity. There are actually five different bonds that form the cord of love in your relationships! These bonds are:

1. The bond of unconditional love.

2. The bond of friendship.

3. The bond of affirmation.

4. The bond of serving.

5. The bond of covering.

The Bond of Unconditional Love

Unconditional love frees us from two terrible fears that keep us from fulfilling our destinies in God: the fear of failure and the fear of rejection. The only way to overcome these twin demons of fear and do anything great for God is to allow unconditional love to set you free! Then you will experience the fullness of the ministry God has for you.

> If I'm not free to fail,
> then I'm not free to succeed.

Every opportunity for success has a corresponding opportunity for failure. If you are afraid you might make a mistake or fail, you won't attempt to do anything for God. Your fear of criticism and rejection by people in the church will keep you from taking the risk.

Opportunity is spelled R-I-S-K. God always arranges opportunities for miracles, but fear will stop you from possessing the miracles God has planned for you. Unconditional love equips us to empower the members of our team to succeed!

Have you ever tried to do something for God, and failed? I have failed so badly that I didn't know if I could ever get up. Do you know what I need to hear when I am down on the ground with my face in the mud of despondency? Let me tell you two responses *I do NOT need to hear*!

1. *I do not need you to tell me what I did wrong.* I know what I did wrong. The devil has been telling me several times a day what I did wrong. In fact, I pretty much believe his lie that not only did I do bad, but I am bad.

2. *I do not need you to tell me what the Bible says about what I did wrong.* I could preach a better sermon about my problems than you could.

The foundation that gives us the "freedom to fail," and thus the freedom to succeed, is unconditional love. We all need someone who will honor, esteem, respect, and value us as much after we fail as he did before we failed. Isn't it true? You need someone to believe in you when you do not even believe in yourself. You need someone to love you when you do not feel lovable! The time you need to be loved the most is when you deserve it the least.

> Unconditional love is a commitment to honor, value, respect, and appreciate each other as much after we fail as we did before.

How can you value someone who just failed? You begin by looking past the temporary event of the failure and seeing the gifts, skills, abilities, life, and strengths that are still there! The failure is an event that is a learning experience, *but it does not determine the value of the person.* It does not stop the person from achieving his destiny.

The Bible says, "For a righteous man falls seven times, and rises again" (Prov. 24:16a). If you fail seven times, how many times do you have to get up? At least seven. It isn't the failure that is important to God—it's the "getting up" that counts!

The bond of unconditional love in our Care Group relationships will cause you to tell me, "Ken, I believe in you. You are still gifted, talented, and strong. I believe you are going to make it. In fact, I know you are going to make it because we are going to go through it together." It will cause you to lay aside judgment for mercy, and reach down and pick me up by your love and faith to walk with me.

I have an odd but important request I want to make of you: "Please make an adequate number of mistakes!" If you are going to reach your destiny, if you are going to succeed in the Care Ministry, *you must make an adequate number of mistakes*. It is part of the learning curve.

I had pastored for 17 years, and when God called me to the traveling ministry, I didn't know anything about how it worked. I made every mistake that anyone had ever made, plus I found some mistakes no one had ever done before! During the first year of this ministry, my learning curve was a vertical line headed straight up, and my income curve was a vertical line plummeting straight down! When my learning curve flattened out, my income line also bottomed out, but life was very difficult that first year.

I could have quit that first year and used my mistakes as a reason to say that God was not blessing the ministry. Of course, I would have also missed my destiny in God! I went through that season of mistakes, I learned, and I allowed those things to improve me and the ministry. Today, we are one of the fastest-growing ministries in the United States! That is why I repeat my exhortation: *"Please make an adequate number of mistakes."* Go out and make the number of mistakes that is needed for you to succeed. If you are not making mistakes, you are not doing the ministry!

Take courage: *The entry level of all ministry is incompetence!* Of course you don't know what you are doing—you are starting at square one. Trust the process of God. As you make mistakes, God will lead you, and He will manage to complete His work in spite of you!

Unconditional love creates a community of encouragement. You need an environment that will strengthen you, not just for the stress and demands from ministry, but for every area of your life. In your career, there will be opportunities that will require risk-taking. When you are empowered by a team of people who love you unconditionally and believe in you, when you have true friends who are there to support you, it will be much easier to "get out of your boat of security" to walk on the water of opportunity!

The Bond of Friendship

When I first started in the pastorate, I discovered that people had expectations about me that went something like this: "Always be in victory, never have any doubts, never have any problems, have answers for every problem in the church, always preach good sermons, and be available when I need you!"

I learned from experience that expectations sabotage relationships! I was a very lonely and isolated pastor. Then I went to a pastor's retreat where a bunch of us decided to play some touch football. The man lined up against me pastored a church of a thousand people. I didn't have a large church, so I knocked him on his fanny! (It felt good.) Then he pulled up some grass and threw it at me, so I threw it right back at him. In seconds, 16 pastors were throwing grass at each other and laughing, carrying on, and having a great time. The best part of it all was this: Right in the middle of that grass fight, while we were being silly and carrying on, *I knew I needed a friend.*

The next Sunday, I told my congregation, "It's awful lonely being on this pastoral pedestal. I've tried to always be in victory, never have any doubts, never have any problems, and never have a down day. Listen, I'm tired of being lonely...if you can accept me just the way I am, with all the good, the bad, and the ugly, warts and all, then we can be friends. I need somebody who will accept me for who and what I am, so I will grow into what God wants me to be." That Sunday was a very liberating day, for I stopped being an institutional pastor and became the friend the church needed me to be. It changed the way I pastored from then on, and it changed the church.

The Bond of Affirmation

Affirmation is the act of seeing good in a person and telling them about it. I learned this principle from a friend named Paul who mentored me in the love of God. He pastored a very large and successful church, yet he treated me in a way that no Christian ever treated me. Every time I got around him, he would tell me how great I was! I had lots of Christians tell me how bad I was, but Paul was different. My friend showed me that there is only one person in the entire universe that wants to see sin, and that's the devil.

About six months after our friendship began, I decided I was going to "out-affirm" Paul. Next time I saw him, I said, "Hi, Paul," and then I affirmed him. Then he affirmed me. Then I affirmed him, and he affirmed me. This went on constantly after that—we became our own Mutual Admiration Society! He was the president and I was the vice-president. I hope you realize that this is the way the church needs to be! What would happen if visitors came to church and all they heard was affirmation and love? They'd think they'd died and gone to Heaven, because after all, *church folk don't talk that way!*

The principle of affirmation says you can only love what you value. Conversely, you cannot love what you do not value. Affirmation and appreciation increase the value of the other person.

Divorce comes from depreciation; love comes from appreciation. This happened in my marriage after Cheryl and I had been married for ten years. We had three kids in three years (once we figured out why, we stopped, but it took us a while). My wife stopped looking like the teenage queen I married ten years earlier, and she began to look like the mother of three children who were all in diapers!

I did what the American male was supposed to do: I began to be critical of my wife. I called it "constructive criticism," but she called it exactly what it was— "criticism."

After this went on for several months, I lost my "warm fuzzies." You have to have warm fuzzies in your marriage, and I didn't have them, so I went to God. I said, "God, I don't have any warm fuzzies in my marriage. What should I do?" He told me to write out a list of the traits and characteristics in Cheryl that had made me want to spend the rest of my life with her ten years earlier.

The list was not performance-based, because if the performance stops, then the love stops. I only listed the traits and characteristics of what and who she is. I listed

47 different traits and characteristics that I valued about Cheryl. Then I asked her, "Honey, do you want to know what I really think about you?" (After several months of my criticism and faultfinding, she hesitated.) Finally, she said, "I guess."

When I read her the list of 47 different traits and characteristics that I valued in her, there were four immediate results: My wife's self-image rose dramatically, she began to develop the values I'd listed that had not yet been fully developed, all the warm fuzzies came back, and Cheryl became my best friend. Honestly, I would rather spend an evening with her than with the President of the United States!

You Have an Appreciation Bucket

You have an "Appreciation Bucket" inside your soul. When you don't receive appreciation, you feel used and empty. Our society is very negative. Very few of us get appreciated at the job, at church, and in our homes. We just don't get our "buckets filled" very often. When someone criticizes you and puts a hole in the bottom of the thing, whatever is inside drains out. We all need to be appreciated, and it takes a conscious decision to relate and communicate in a changed lifestyle.

The Care Ministry, and the Christian life in general, requires a lifestyle of affirmation, a lifestyle of seeing good in people and telling them about it. Psychologists claim that 77 percent of what we think about ourselves is negative! Maybe it is no accident that we have a difficult time seeing good in ourselves, much less others. People need 14 hugs a day to remain emotionally stable. Some of you thought you had a real problem, but all you need is more hugs each day.

The Bond of Serving

John the apostle wrote, "We know love by this, that He laid down His life for us; and we ought to lay down our lives for the brethren" (1 Jn. 3:16). Serving is one of the most powerful demonstrations of love you can give someone in need. Serving gives people your time, a precious commodity that cannot be replaced. Serving is *love in action.*

Mary came to church because of a big need. Her mother, Alice, had been admitted to the hospital for a major operation. Mary desperately wanted prayer, so when the prayer request card was handed out, she eagerly poured out her concern over her mother's need in the hospital. That week she received a call from Bill, the staff person she met at church. He wasn't a stranger, so when he told her that he and the entire staff, including the senior pastor, had prayed for her mother, it strengthened her faith.

Bill did not stop with the prayer. He asked how her mother was doing, and then he asked if he could visit her in the hospital. Mary was overwhelmed by the love and care she was receiving, and was excited about how her unsaved mother would respond. That same week,

Arnie, the Care Team leader, also called Mary and told her that he and his wife had been praying for her all week long. Then he also asked if he and some friends could visit her mother.

By the end of the week, Alice had received ministry from Pastor Bill and all the members of Arnie's Care Team. Each time they prayed for her, she felt her condition immediately improve. She had never experienced anything like that before. When she told her daughter, Mary, what happened, they both cried. The next Sunday Mary was back in church. Within a month, her unsaved mother was saved and in church too. Why? They were *served* in their time of need.

The Bond of Covering

The Bible says that "love covers a multitude of sins" (1 Pet. 4:8). If you are going to minister with and to other believers, you must understand the bond of covering! As you minister and fellowship together, you are sure to see the sins, faults, and weaknesses of others. When we cover sin, mistakes, and failures with the love of God, it frees us from the fear of backbiting and gossip that destroys the faith we need to succeed.

Chapter 6

Care Groups, Team Ministry, and You!

My daughter, Beth, played varsity on a basketball team that went to the state tournament each of the four years she was there. In her freshman year, the team placed second in the state. The next year, they won third place; and in her junior year, they were fourth in the state. By her senior year, Beth had a passion and a goal to see her team win the state championship. The only way to satisfy her desire was to win the state title—nothing less would do. Unfortunately, they had to beat a crosstown rival that had beaten her team in five consecutive games over the previous two years!

This time, Beth's coach changed his strategy for the state tournament: He kept the starting five in the game and played them every minute. By doing so, he acciden-tally released the power of a unified vision! Each of those girls had shared the same burning vision for four years, yet the championship level of *relationships in trust and bonding* did not occur until the coach made his de-cision to keep all of them together to the end.

I was looking for something in the players' eyes be-fore the game, and when I looked at my daughter, I saw it! There was fire in her eyes and confidence in her shot—she wasn't missing a hoop. The entire team had the confidence of the passion being fulfilled *because the members of the team had confidence in each other*!

Right then I knew we were going to have a great game. Beth didn't miss a shot in the first half, and she led both teams in scoring and rebounding, and she led her team to a halftime lead. In the second half, the other members of the team stepped up their game too. In the end, the team that had beaten them five times in the past two years was no match for this fiery group of girls *that became a team.*

Unfortunately, most churches do not give their members the opportunity to be champions or to expe-rience that type of fulfillment because they do not structure the ministry into *team ministry.* God wants you to be a champion on His team, but you must first *be on a team* to be a champion. He wants all of us to discover, as my daughter did, that a higher level of effectiveness and power comes when we are bonded together with others in love and trust for a common vision! Jesus formed a ministry team and turned the world upside down. He is out to do it *again!*

What Is Care Team Ministry?

The Care Team Ministry isn't radical or new—it is a biblical model Jesus gave us with the 12 apostles. Jesus did not attempt to do the ministry by Himself; His first step into ministry was to recruit 12 ordinary men. He discipled them, related to them, and imparted His vision and goals to them. That ministry team turned the world upside down. The apostle Paul never attempted a missionary journey by himself either. He always had a team.

Most pastors and full-time ministers live near the edge of burnout most of their lives because the "system" is backwards. They went to seminary or Bible school to be "equipped" for the ministry *so they could do it all,* just like their boards and congregations expect them to! The Church has stopped following the biblical model that Jesus gave for ministry—and we wonder why the Church is not effective. We are doing it the wrong way. When the other biblical model, cell groups, was revived in the Church in recent years, pastors around the world eagerly instituted them. Their hope was that the cell group would meet the needs of the members and produce the growth seen in the Bible. The cell groups did not produce growth because they are only maintenance structures. Cell groups do not have the dynamics of team ministry. Many pastors gave up on cell groups because they wanted growth and got maintenance for two to three years before the groups died.

How to Transform a Group Into a Team

The Care Team takes the cell group to a higher level of ministry by transforming the group into a ministry team. A Care Team is two or more people bonded together with a common *vision*, and *relating* together to achieve common *goals*. The vision is the bond and the passion of the team. The team is not bonded together by being a homogeneous grouping. The vision bonds and motivates them for ministry and not for themselves. The transformation from cell group to Care Team simply requires that the leader have a vision of the Care Team producing growth; that the leader be retrained to lead a Care Team; that those group members who want to minister be trained and equipped with the ministry skills to meet the needs of first-time attenders; and that the church implements Care Team Ministry strategies, systems, and structures to assimilate the first-time attenders into the church.

Very few saints are being trained and equipped with the ministry skills to effectively meet the needs of others; if they are, they lack the dynamics of team ministry that Jesus gave to His disciples. Personal growth and church growth occur best within the environment of a Care Team where the members share a vision of meeting the needs of others by the power of the Spirit, of personally making disciples, and of building relationships that will bond everyone together to fulfill the mission!

The next generation of cell groups is team ministry. Why? The Lord is taking group relationships to a higher level of ministry to produce disciples for Jesus.

If you want to be personally productive and release all your gifts, strengths, skills, and the life of God within you, then you need to be on a Care Team! Independent ministry won't fulfill you; being dependent on the pastor for your spiritual life won't mature you. Interdependency with other Care Team members is the way God structured His Kingdom for you to be fulfilled and experience the miracles God has for you. You need the strengths of others to cover your weaknesses. You also need the love and support of your team to strengthen and encourage your faith. You will never experience all that God created you to be without having team ministry. The Care Ministry will release the power of team ministry into your life and the life of the church.

If that seems like a shocking statement, then put yourself into the well-worn shoes of the overworked, exhausted pastors throughout the world who have sensed the purpose of God for their ministry when I told them,

"Pastor, when you implement the Care Ministry in your church, you will no longer be doing the ministry by yourself or just with your staff. Rather, you will be on a team. In fact, the Care Teams will be composed of the 20 percent or more of the people in your church who catch the vision to minister to needs of the visitors and disciple them into the church." Church leaders are excited to finally discover the ministry strategy, systems, and structure that will:

- Transform church members into champions for the Lord.

- Transform maintenance groups into growth-producing Care Teams.

- Transform church members into assimilators to relationally shut the "back door."

- Transform the visitation program into a discipleship and assimilation ministry.

- Transform growth into revival.

- Transform addition into multiplication.

The Bible does not support the current model of "one-man ministry," either by the pastor for the church, or the cell leader for the group. (From the very beginning, Jesus put His disciples directly into one-on-one ministry situations after He had trained them.)

There's a Champion inside you wanting to be released. His name is Jesus. But you don't have the opportunity to become God's champion because you are struggling by yourself in the ministry. You need the power released by the Care Team Ministry. Not only are you struggling, but there are countless "champions" in your local church who have no opportunity to become God's champions because they too have been struggling in ministry by themselves.

Biblical Care Ministry positions the local church as an equipping center with dynamic and productive Care Teams that produce spiritual champions! My friend, Darrell Massier, led 500 people to the Lord and reproduced Care Group leaders eight times in five years! How did he do it? Darrell was on a Care Team and he had relationships and a vision that gave him the passion to lead his team during the evangelistic events the church sponsored. Those events and monthly Sunday ministry gave his team the ideal target group to minister to. Darrell became a champion for the Lord because he was on a Care Team dedicated to making disciples and assimilating them into their small group. The reason Darrell's group multiplied eight times in six years is because his group was a team with a vision that changed the lives of the Care Team members.

Every *Care Ministry* has four or more *Care Teams.* (The number of teams is determined by the number of visitors.) At the core of every Care Group is a Care Team, composed of trained and motivated believers who release their faith, prayers, and lives to build up others. When the first-time attenders they are reaching, assimilating, and discipling join the Care Team members for regular "equipping" meetings, then you have a *Care Group*. The synergy of these teams of men and women with a common vision produces faith to achieve their dream. Their common goals give them the hope to keep working for the next step. Their rich relationships give them love and bonding that empower them to experience a higher level of the Christian life!

There are three progressive steps to the Care Team ministry: the "In-Church Ministry"; the "Pursuit Ministry"; and the "Assimilation Ministry." The Care Team embraces the total ministry vision of lovingly bringing the first-time attender into a long-term, two-way family relationship with the body of believers we call the church; and it does it by meeting needs. The unique (and biblical) aspect of the Care Team ministry is that this ministry to visitors is no longer a "staff responsibility." Once again, this vital "work of service" ("work of the ministry" in the King James Version) is being accomplished by the people God clearly indicates can most effectively do it: the members or "saints" of the local church.

Seeing the End From the Beginning

The Care Ministry is driven by *relationships*. Caring relationships are the most effective means we have to bond visitors to the church body. Members of Care Teams invest themselves exclusively in one visitor or visiting family at a time, to properly minister to their needs, build relationships, and become their "bridge" into the life of the local church. This process normally takes between one and two months.

Perhaps the greatest strength of Care Ministry is that it is based on God's vision of redemption. In other words, *we see the end from the beginning.* Just as God began our salvation process long before we ever surrendered to Him as Lord and Savior, we must start the "assimilation process" on the first Sunday visitors attend the local church service. That can only be done when the visitor's relational and spiritual needs are met by Care Team members who are trained to care and minister by the Spirit of God. From the moment visitors step through the door, we *see them* as miracles disguised as needs. We see beyond the outward appearance and perceive that they are *miracles waiting to happen!*

Team Ministry Assimilates Into the Group

Hard experience has shown that visitors need seven friends within six months or they are out the back door of the church! That is why Care Teams begin the friendship process the very first Sunday visitors come. The Care Team is the small group to reach out, love, minister to, and accept the first-time attender! One of our most important goals is for the first-time attender to meet everyone on the Care Team the very first Sunday he attends. Why? When he returns the next week, the Care Team knows who he is. They go out of their way to give him the loving attention that makes him feel important (because he *is important*). This removes the ugly stigma of "visitor" and "stranger," and makes him feel like he *belongs*.

This consistent attention and loving care from the Care Team provides a naturally appealing invitation for first time attenders to more actively relate to the group on a more intimate and frequent level. The number one objection visitors have to attending small group meetings is, "I'm not going to go to a group *full of strangers*." When a Care Group is involved, visitors are not being invited to a meeting with strangers; they are being invited to spend more time with the caring, loving people who have already invested personal attention and ministry in their lives. The members of the Care Team have "paid the price" of love and "earned the right" to invite the visitor to spend more time with them.

The last time the visitor is *contacted by a stranger* should be the first Sunday he attends your church. From the first warm word of greeting by a Care Team member and onward, the visitor begins to meet more "friends of his friend" as he meets the other Team members and pastoral staff the first Sunday. These *relationships* turn the insignificant "touches by strangers" into *emotional deposits by friends*.

Personal contact and ministry are only effective when they are offered by a friend, not a stranger. The Care Team members are determined to minister to visitors until they become part of the group. They understand that they must *invest* in the visitors' needs to earn the right to minister to them and assimilate them into the church.

This type of ministry cannot be done by small groups who are told, "Your ministry now includes being friendly at church on Sunday. That means you need to invite visitors to your group." Why not? The problem is that the typical church home group or cell group has a vision and purpose to maintain those who are already attending the meeting. There is nothing wrong with this goal, but it will never produce growth and maturity in the members of the group because they are not being equipped for the work of service God intended for them! If you introduce the need for outreach and new vision to existing cell groups, only part of the group will "buy into the new definition and vision." The remainder will be frustrated that the attention has been taken away from them. They may even attempt to sabotage the new vision.

We have also learned that without training, cell group members will not know how to minister to visitors. The strategy behind the Care Ministry will be partially understood, but the ministry itself will be ineffective because the members won't know what to say or do with visitors. The end of this frustrating exercise will be that outgoing members of each cell group will continue to reach out, while the rest will only "give it a try." When they inevitably have an unpleasant experience, they will vow to never do it again, saying, "It's not my ministry." The problem isn't the wrong ministry, but inadequate training.

In-Church Care Team Ministry

One of the greatest misconceptions restricting the growth of local churches is the way they view visitors. They tend to approach visitors with the ultimate purpose of discovering *how the visitor can meet the needs of the church*! As a result of this skewed perspective of visitors, the church and church staff unknowingly offer preferential treatment to the more educated, talented, and prosperous visitors. Others who "don't have as much to offer" do not get the same attention—if they get any attention at all!

The fact is that visitors are not "objects to be used for the good of the church." Visitors are miracles disguised as needs. When you see visitors only for "what they can do for your church," you have a wrong motive. You only want to "use them for your benefit" instead of "serving them for their blessing." The church that meets the most needs will be the church that grows the fastest and nurtures what they have received!

Every visitor needs the "Two A's"—attention and anonymity. It doesn't seem very fair to ask for *both* of them, does it? Fair or not, they need both. Visitors want to feel important to us, and they want to feel like we care, but they don't want to stick out and be different! No, they want to blend in and be like everyone else. Most churches give visitors attention all right—by publicly branding them with a tag like a head of beef in a livestock auction ring! So much for anonymity. Care Teams avoid public embarrassment by quietly and privately identifying visitors in their assigned seating sections every week.

It's hard to accept, but now we know the last thing we should do to first-time attenders is slap a badge on their lapel that says, "I am a visitor." So *what should we do?* We are going to meet them personally and protect their anonymity. The in-church ministry of the Care Team is to identify the visitors in the sanctuary or foyer, and to give them the quality of personal care, attention, and communication that will be effective enough to earn the right to minister to them.

The Care Team's objective is to make "deposits of care and love" instead of "withdrawals through the touch of a stranger." The Care Ministry does not *contact*; it *impacts* by the power of the love of God. We need to earn the right to see visitors during the week in their homes. When we care more about meeting our visitors' needs than our own, then they will want to come back because of the love they received from the Care Team.

Every member of a Care Team is looking for hurting people who need the ministry of the love and power of God. When one Care Team member identifies a first-time attender, the entire Care Team is immediately told the name of the visitor and where he is seated. That helps to ensure that the entire Care Team will meet *every visitor* to each service, although one Care Team member or couple will specifically minister to each visitor and begin to develop a caring friendship. A Care Team leader coordinates these ministry efforts and carefully searches the congregation for other visitors or ministry needs.

The Link Between the Pulpit and the Pew

The only way the Care Ministry will be effective is if it works as part of the larger ministry team of the church, under the leadership of the local pastor. We recommend that the senior pastor always personally and publicly welcome the visitors. Why? The pastor is the most important *servant* in the church, and what he does and says is important. When an associate pastor welcomes the visitors, it may be perceived as a statement that visitors are not important enough to merit the senior pastor's time or attention. On the other hand, when the pastor personally welcomes visitors, that says to the entire church—and to the visitors—that first-time attenders are important to him and to the church. What would *you think* if you visited a church and heard the senior pastor say something like this:

"We want to welcome all first-time attenders who are here today. You are not here by accident, but by appointment. You see, we have prayed for you to be here today! God brought you here because He wants to work a miracle in your life, and He wants us to help you find your miracle.

"If you would fill out the First-Time Attender Prayer Request Card, then our staff will pray for you on Tuesday, and we also have a team of believers who will pray for you *personally, every day this week!* We want you to know you are not alone with your needs any longer. You are not alone with your problems. We are here for you to find God's miracles for your life.

"We are a very friendly church. So don't be surprised if you have people lining up to meet you— we care about you, and you are important to us. In fact, don't be surprised if you are invited out for Sunday dinner—just go and get a free meal! And don't be surprised if someone wants to pray for you. We believe God answers prayers, and we want to see God bless your life."

The Care Ministry carefully matches up men with men, women with women, and singles with singles. In many cases, we even try to match races and ethnic groups to better build a bridge into the church body. We need to make this "human bridge" as close to the visitor as possible to lower any obstacles that might be there. Ultimately, our goal is to eliminate all obstacles into our fellowship.

Post-Service Care Team Objectives

Once a Care Team has the name and the location of the visitors, their goal is to minister to them after the church service. During the benediction, the Care Team members will leave their seats in the back row where they have been silently interceding for the visitors during the service. At the "amen," they will go into the row while everyone else is going out, because we have found that if we can meet first-time attenders in the row right then, they will spend a few minutes with us.

Another reason we meet them immediately after service is because we will never know who the "divine appointment" is unless we make contact with every visitor. We believe God is bringing someone to the church each week who is part of the harvest, and we won't know who the miracle is unless we make contact with 100 percent of the visitors.

The Fifteen Percent Rule

The Care Ministry is an aggressive ministry. We are aggressively looking for the divine appointment. We are aggressively looking for the miracle God has birthed in prayer before the service. We are aggressively looking for the person with the need we are to minister to. When we find that person, he is always happy we were aggressive!

However, as we contact each of the first-time attenders, we will also find the 15 percent of the visitors who do not want our attention! Why do I say "15 percent"? Church growth studies indicate that churches retain about 15 percent of their visitors. That means 15 percent of the visitors will probably like your church, love the pastor, love the message, and think this is the friendliest church they ever attended—even if you stick a visitor's tag on them! They already want to talk to somebody about the church.

On the other end of the response spectrum, there is "another 15 percent" who don't like the church, don't like the pastor, got nothing out of the message, and can't believe how unfriendly the church is! The odd thing about it is that both families attended the same service! These folks can't wait to get out of church, and they don't want to talk to anybody. They definitely don't want any more contact from this horrible church.

This is the group that has inspired most of the "myths" about visitors. If you dare to contact them after church, they will tell you they don't like anybody to bother them. If you "follow up" on them later on, they may even be rude. That is how many people have concluded that "visitors don't want to be bothered. Leave them alone." The people who will never come back to your church don't want to be bothered, but 85 percent of the people who want to come back, or who are thinking about coming back, really want personal care and attention. They long for personal ministry, and they want our love.

Anyone who truly wants to be effective in discovering the miracles God is sending to them will also find those who have a negative response. Don't allow 15 percent of the visitors to dictate or limit the ministry and love you give to the 85 percent who come to your church looking for their needs to be met!

Chapter 7

Experience Miracles
Every Sunday

Lee stood alone by the coatrack in the foyer of the church, trying to decide if he really wanted to go into the sanctuary. Everyone he saw was well-dressed, and they all looked successful. Lee felt exactly the opposite way about himself. He had come to church in blue jeans and a two-days' growth of beard. Now he was feeling out of place in this building with all these successful, attractive-looking people. He felt anything but successful.

Lee had just lost his job and his girlfriend. He was so discouraged that he was seriously thinking about suicide. He had just decided that he did not want to go in and risk being ignored; but before he could make a hasty exit, Marty showed up! He came right up to Lee with a friendly, disarming smile and a personal approach that invited Lee to like him. He said, "Hi, my name is Marty. What's your name?" Lee responded automatically, amazed that someone actually wanted to talk to him in the foyer: "My name is Lee."

"How long have you been coming to Bloomington?" Marty asked. Lee immediately felt comfortable with Marty, so he said, "This is my first time here, but I was thinking of leaving." Marty showed no sign of disapproval, only concern. He asked Lee, "Why do you want to leave, Lee?" Then he listened intently when Lee told him he felt out of place and uncomfortable. Marty made Lee feel good about being there, and he was so interested in Lee that he decided not to leave. In fact, Lee began to tell him about the battles he was having with discouragement and thoughts of suicide.

Marty realized that what Lee needed was a personal relationship with Jesus Christ. He asked Lee if he had a relationship with the Lord Jesus, and he said he didn't know. Right there in the foyer of the church by the coatrack, Lee received the Lord Jesus into his heart. Not only did Lee go to church that morning, but he became part of the church–blue jeans, beard, and all!

Hurting people like Lee are finding salvation and healing in churches across America because anointed Care Team members are coming to church services with a spirit of expectancy! They are looking for people who need a miracle from the Lord! This can be your testimony too. All you have to do is become part of a Care Team ministry and follow a simple Bible-based ministry strategy for the "in-church ministry."

Care Team Ministry Overview

Care Teams typically minister one Sunday per month. They use the rest of the month to continue to meet the needs of the visitors they befriend during their "Ministry Sunday." If you commit to serve the Lord on a Care Team, you will minister from 15 to 20 minutes before the church service, and about the same amount of time afterward. Each time, you will work to achieve three pre-service ministry objectives and six post-service ministry objectives. Your Care Team will be careful to minister *as a team* to avoid placing all the ministry responsibilities on one person.

Once a visitor has received ministry in a church service and leaves, then your Care Team will continue to minister to that visitor through the "Pursuit Ministry" until he bonds to the Care Group and is assimilated into the local church family.

Care Team members don't limit their preparation and ministry to the time they are in a church building, though. Caring isn't something you do; it's something within you that you *are*, manifesting in a lifestyle of care! Care Team ministers look for miracles in their homes and in grocery stores during the week, and they prepare for miracles before they ever get to the church building. When they gather in unified prayer before a church service, they jointly take three important steps to "release the team anointing" of God upon their need-fulfillment ministry!

First Goal: Release the Team Anointing

Thirty minutes before the church service, the team meets together in prayer and unity to accomplish three vital purposes.

1. *Stir up the love of God.* Everyone on the team will exchange hugs, tell one another how they love each other, and generally show appreciation for each other. We must do that so when we enter the sanctuary, the love of God is already flowing among us. We will simply give to others what we have received from our team members in Christ. If you don't stir up the love of God within your team, you will not have the love and openness necessary to bond a visitor to you.

2. *Release the spirit of faith.* "Faith is the switch that turns on the power." The team members will confess faith to each other in agreement with God's Word so their level of faith will increase. Remember, attitude determines altitude. Most people live in the altitude of mediocrity, but God wants us to live in the altitude of miracles. The only way

to get to the higher altitude is by faith. If miracles are going to occur, they will happen because our team is walking in the spirit of faith, fully expecting to see God move!

3. *Review the ministry strategy.* Your team leader will walk through the objectives for "pre-service ministry," the announcements, and the "post-service ministry," and will assign your designated ministry area in the sanctuary.

Work the Crowd in the Spirit

Once the Care Team has been released to minister, they immediately begin "working" (or serving) the crowd, looking for *divine appointments* where needs will meet their miracles by the Spirit of God! This "pre-service" ministry takes place wherever the people are, whether it is in the sanctuary, the hallway, or by a coatrack in the foyer! Every Care Team member is passionately looking for visitors who came to church needing God! In effect, we are "starting church before church starts." We believe the Holy Spirit wants to meet needs where we find them! We make ourselves available for a miracle by pursuing four key objectives before the church service begins.

Pre-Service Ministry Objectives

1. *Make the church more friendly.* Within the first 11 minutes of their visit in your church building,

visitors will decide whether or not they will be coming back. That means they have made their decision *long before* your pastor can impress them with his preaching, or shake their hand at the end of the service! How we serve them prior to church will communicate to them whether they are important to us. How many people walked out of your church this last year *convinced you did not care for them?*

Those first 11 minutes are so critical that the Care Team Ministry must even extend to the church parking lot! You should assign a designated *visitor parking* area in view of the front doors so the greeters at the door can identify visitors before they enter. After the greeters introduce themselves to the visitors, they will escort them to a hospitality table where Care Group members are waiting to give them some material and escort them wherever they need to go (whether it is the nursery, children's church, or some other specific service the church provides for the family). The Care Group members will also take them back to the sanctuary where the Care Team is ministering and personally introduce them.

2. *Each visitor will be greeted by every Team Member.* When the team "working" the crowd sees Care Members escorting visitors into the sanctuary,

they make sure the visitors are greeted by each member of the team. Any team member who identifies a visitor quickly notifies the team leader and the other members of the team. It is easy for team members to identify visitors because each member "works one section" in the sanctuary. When you minister to a visitor, make sure to take the next step: Round up everyone on your team and make sure each person talks to the visitor you met.

3. *Make friends with visitors.* Remember that a visitor needs seven friends in six months, or they are out the back door. Your Care Ministry goal is to make sure every visitor in your section makes at least one new friend the first Sunday he comes. Who is the new friend? You are! The bonds of relationship you form serve two important purposes. First, they help you meet visitors' needs. Most people only share their needs with someone they trust, not with strangers. Second, we know that anointed "pulpit ministry" will draw people to the church, but it is *personal relationship* that *keeps them there!*

4. *Pray for three people.* As you work the crowd before the service begins, look for the "seven signs of hurting people." When you discern that someone is hurting, stop and pray for them. I don't care if

they are a member or a visitor, you are there to meet needs, so pray. The average Care Team is made up of ten people plus the team leader. When every team member prays for three people, that means 30 people will receive ministry! The Care Ministry will discover more divine appointments by accident than the average church will find on purpose!

The Seven Signs of Hurting People

We have noticed seven outward indicators of a hurt or wounded spirit that provide a pretty accurate warning signal of a need seeking a miracle. Every Care Team minister should study these and pray over them before every ministry service to prepare his heart and sharpen his discernment.

1. *People's countenances.* The countenance or appearance of the human face reveals the condition of the soul within. You can see a drawn and oppressed face, and you can usually interpret body language very accurately. As a Care Team minister, you are looking for hurt in people, not sin. You're looking for pain in the countenance when working the crowd.

2. *People's eyes, which are the window of the soul.* Are the visitor's eyes bright and alive, or are they dull and empty? Can you see hurt, loneliness, or heartache in those eyes?

3. *People sitting alone.* When people sit in a church service alone, whether they are single, a couple, or an entire family, their physical isolation indicates that they don't have any friends in the church. It also indicates that they don't know anybody in the church, and no one knows them. They probably feel like nobody loves or cares about them as well. They need to feel important to *somebody.*

4. *People with their heads down.* People who bow their heads down when no one is praying are probably reading their Bible for one of two reasons: Either they haven't read it all week long and they're trying to catch up, or they are avoiding eye contact! If they're avoiding eye contact, they may be afraid they will be rejected if they make contact with anyone. Nobody wants to come to church and feel rejected. Politely "interrupt" the reader by coming close enough for him to know you are there. When the visitor looks up, the first thing he will see is your *smile.* The first thing he will hear is your warm greeting, "Hi, I'm Ken. What's your name?"

5. *People new to your section.* We are creatures of habit. When you come to church, you're going to work your section *every* Sunday, not just your "Ministry Sunday." Within a month you will know

the favorite seats and names of all the regular people in your section. You will know where the uninvolved people sit who come once or twice a month, and *you will know those visitors!*

6. *People who act tentatively.* If you see people in the foyer acting like they don't know where they're going, do not assume that "someone else" will take care of them. *You do it.* Go up to them and ask, "Can I help you?" If they don't know where the children's ministry is, you take them. If they don't know where the nursery is, you take them. Don't wait for the greeters or ushers to do it. You do it!

7. *People who sit in the back.* Visitors tend to sit in the aisles near the back (so they can run out in case of an emergency!). People "on their way out" sit in the back. Discover the mission field—look at the back two or three rows at church next Sunday! People who are thinking about leaving the church are back there.

Sanctuary Ministry in Action

On your monthly "Ministry Sunday," you will sit on an aisle seat of the back row so you can pick up the prayer request cards during the announcements. Once you have saved your seat on the back row, you begin to ask the Lord to show you who He wants you to minister to as you walk down the aisle and look out over the sanctuary.

When I first went on staff at a very large church, I did not know very many of the 4,000 people who attended there. I decided to "work the crowds" before and after the service to get to know people. I would approach people with a smile and say, "Hi, my name is Ken Houts. What's your name? God bless you." I did that for three weeks. I skipped the fourth week and then began the process again the next week. When I greeted the same people, to my amazement, they told me they missed me greeting them! They missed a simple smile and "God bless you." They missed the attention.

I did not realize it, but I was the only staff pastor who would leave the platform before church to be friendly with the congregation. The other pastors wondered what in the world I was doing! I wasn't praying for people, but I *was* ministering to them—by being friendly, by smiling, and by blessing them. Pretty soon the senior pastor had the entire staff out working the crowd before church!

The first thing people are going to see is your smile. Smiles invite people to feel comfortable with you. I like to start smiling before I get to a person. The Bible says, "Death and life are in the power of the tongue" (Prov. 18:21a). You can release blessing on your church if you go around smiling at people and saying, "God bless you." If that's all you can do, then you're being a great success in the Care Ministry. The reason the folks missed me when I did not greet them involved much more than missing a friendly smile—they were missing the extra measure of life and blessings from God that came through the spoken blessings of a believer.

While you work the crowds, smiling and blessing people, also look for pain. You are looking for hurt, and when you find it, you will stop and minister. When you feel that you know whom the Lord wants you to pray for, do not go directly to that person. Begin to be friendly to people near them so they will anticipate your friendly ministry to them. Then it will only be natural to begin a conversation with that person. Since ministry is always most effective when it comes from a friend, you first want to become a friend. After you introduce yourself and learn their name, begin to ask questions about their life, their interests, and their feelings. At first, you will only discover facts about their life, but then you must progress to their needs and motivation for coming to church.

As you talk with the visitor, you will also carry on a private conversation with the Holy Spirit. You are asking the Lord which of the "seven conditions of hurting sheep" this person has. (The way you know those "seven conditions" is by reviewing them that morning before the church service ever begins. See pages 40 through 44 for the list.) Now the Lord has something He can quicken in your mind as you talk to the person.

As you listen to the visitor, you may also sense the Holy Spirit showing you that this person is confused about some circumstances in her life. "She doesn't know exactly which way to go. She's discouraged about it and she feels like she's fighting this thing by herself. She's lonely." At that point, it is appropriate to ask, "Is there anything I can pray about with you?" If she says, "No, I can't think of anything I need prayer for," then you probably haven't earned the right for her to trust you with her pain. Don't let that stop you from continuing the ministry.

Your first response should be to smile. Then say, "You know, I believe God answers prayer. I felt strongly that God wants to bless you today. Do you believe God answers prayer? Let's pray together, because I believe God wants to bless you today." Then take her by the hand and pray. Go ahead and pray against the confusion you sensed by the Spirit. Pray that the Lord would give her wisdom, direction, encouragement, and the faith to walk this thing through. End the prayer with a smile and thank her for letting you pray for her.

"What if I missed God? What if she wasn't confused or discouraged, and everything's fine? What if she'd had the best week of her life?" The worst thing that can happen is that the person will be blessed by your love and care, no matter how misguided your prayer may be. And you will be blessed because you dared to step out in faith and obedience to God. Even if you miss it, this is a "win-win" situation! The safest way to do this is to just obey and pray.

Mid-Service Announcements

The senior pastor will personally welcome visitors at the beginning of the announcements midway through the service with a positive, loving greeting: "We want to welcome all first-time attenders here today. You are here, not by accident, *but by appointment!* You are here because we have prayed for you to be here today. We believe God wants to do a miracle in your life and He wants us to help you find that miracle. Help us by filling out a prayer request card when the ushers pass them down your row. We're going to ask God to do a miracle in your life!"

The ushers will pass out the cards, and the pastor will ask the visitors to pass the cards to the center aisle after the announcements so the Care Team members can pick them up. The "First-Time Attender Prayer Request" card has a place where you can write the exact location of the visitor's seat before you take it back to the team leader waiting in the foyer.

When the team leader distributes the cards to his team members, he matches up the visitors with Care Team members who are most like them. He will give each team member the bottom portion of the NCR (no carbon required) First-Time Attender Prayer Request Card, and the top portion goes to the office (we developed this format specifically for the Care Ministry). The team leader begins the "tracking system" at this point to make sure each visitor receives consistent care for the next month or so. Then the Team will return to the sanctuary.

Post-Service Ministry

Occasionally a visitor will "slip through" the care network, or someone will minister to him before the service but fail to notify the rest of the Care Team. If you did not make contact with a first-time attender before church, then you *have to* make contact with that person at the end of the service. You will not find miracles unless you talk personally to people and pray with them *before they leave church.* You cannot be a person's friend unless you make personal contact with him before he leaves church!

The first Sunday a visitor comes to church should be the last Sunday he is contacted by a "stranger" from that church! We don't want visitors to talk to "strangers" from our church. We don't want them contacted by "strangers" from our church. We don't want them to know a "stranger" in our church after that first Sunday. Why? Because we were all transformed *from strangers to friends that first Sunday!* You've got to make contact with these people that first Sunday! The most important elements in the Care Ministry are personal involvement, personal care, and personal ministry—and that just won't happen if we are perceived as strangers!

Post-Benediction Introduction

As a minister, you must sometimes break with tradition. You must leave your seat in the back during the benediction, and quietly walk down the aisle to the row where the visitor is seated. Right at the final "Amen," you need to go right into the row *when everyone else is leaving!* Why should you be so "aggressive" in ministry? First, it is a fact that once visitors "hit the aisle," they are gone! Once they are in motion, they won't want to talk to you. However, if you can get inside the row and meet them there, they will probably spend between five and ten minutes with you.

Second, you must be aggressive because you don't know *who the miracle is,* and you won't know unless you and the other team members talk to *every visitor.* Personal contact is the only way to have a divine appointment, so if you don't get to minister to a visitor before church, then go after him after the service. It is imperative, for souls and eternal destinies are on the line! The Care Ministry stands or falls on *personal ministry* on Sunday morning. It won't work if it doesn't happen. Anything less than 100 percent contact and connection with first-time attenders before they leave is "less than you can do."

If you connect with a visitor before church and a relationship is building that you feel good about, then tell your leader. You may have connected with somebody in another section, but just tell the leader, "I talked with Joe Visitor over there, and we have the same interests and the same things in common. I think it would be really good if I was with him." The leader will see that you get that visitor's prayer card.

You also need to keep five "post-service ministry objectives" in mind as you approach the end of a church service. They set the stage for dynamic, impacting ministry that will literally change lives forever!

Five Post-Service Ministry Objectives

1. *Make a friend.*

2. *Pray for him.*

3. *Introduce him to the Care Team leader.* This is important because the team leader will be calling the visitors that week, and it *must* be a personal contact, not a "stranger" contact. When you introduce the Care leader to the visitors, the visitors will value the team leader as you do. They do not know him at that point, but by your sharing your relationship and appreciation for the leader, they will value him too.

4. *Introduce him to the pastor.* Do the same thing with the pastor. When you personally take visitors to

the pastor, he won't have to run around and find them. He will get to meet every single visitor because the Care Team has accepted the responsibility to personally take them to him. Again, when you express your love and respect for your pastor to the visitors, they will automatically take your cue and view the pastor the same way. This will help when he makes one of the "seven deposits of ministry" that week too, because he won't be a stranger calling a stranger anymore!

5. *Make an appointment to see him in his home that week.*

Chapter 8

The Power
of Pursuit Ministry

It was a cold, snowy Monday night in January when Darrell and Mary went on the "Cookie Crusade." Six inches of snow had already fallen, and there was a sheet of ice on the roads, which made traveling difficult. Mary asked Darrell, "Are you sure we need to go tonight?" Darrell was firm in his conviction that they were about to encounter a *divine appointment* with Martha, a first-time attender (but he had no idea how much of an adventure they were heading for). They carefully drove the 25 miles across town to Martha's house.

When Darrell and Mary arrived, Martha and her husband were surprised they had come to visit them on such a difficult night. It obviously impressed both the husband, Bill, who answered the door, and Martha, the first-time attender. Darrell mentioned the prayer request card as a beginning point, since it had noted such an obvious need: Martha had cancer.

"I Prayed Someone Would Help Me"

Martha explained to Darrell and Mary that she had been raised as a Roman Catholic, and initially she had gone to her priest about her cancer, seeking prayer and help. The priest talked to her about getting "right with the church," but he would not attempt to meet her need. (I realize that not all Roman Catholic priests would react this way.) After that, Martha attended several other churches, hoping to find help, but no one would reach out to her. She said, "I finally found out about your church from a friend, and I prayed someone would help me."

Darrell responded to her heartfelt need by saying, "Martha, the reason Mary and I came here tonight in the middle of this snowstorm is because we care about you. And we believe God wants to meet every need you have. God loves you and wants the best for you. We are here because we believe God wanted us to be with you tonight, and because God knows your need, and He wants to meet it."

"I can understand why you are worried, Martha," Darrell continued. "Cancer is a serious and scary disease. Times like these make us begin to evaluate our lives, and they give us a different perspective about life, don't they?" Martha nodded and said, "That has been happening to me ever since the doctor told me about the cancer and the operation."

"That's What I've Been Looking For!"

"Let me ask you a question," Darrell said. "If you would die tonight, do you know for certain you would go to Heaven?" Martha responded tentatively, "I don't think so." Then Darrell asked, "Would you like to have that assurance and to have a relationship with God?" Then Martha said, "That's what I've been looking for!"

As Darrell led Martha through the Scriptures that lay the groundwork for a personal relationship with the Lord, Martha often had objections from her past religious training, but Mary was silently interceding against the religious confusion. Mary noticed that Martha's husband, Bill, didn't have any objections to the things Darrell was teaching from the Scriptures. He kept nodding his head in agreement with Darrell. As Darrell continued to share the Word, Martha's countenance changed and she began to believe what the Bible had to say about her needs.

When Darrell asked Martha if she wanted to receive Jesus Christ as her personal Lord, both she and Bill wanted to pray. So Darrell and Mary had the joy of leading both Bill and Martha to the Lord on that cold, snowy night in January.

Darrell then prayed for Martha's healing, but now her attitude had changed because she realized Darrell and Mary were there to meet her need, not to "get anything" from her. Martha told Darrell, "When you prayed for me, I felt the love of God in a way I had never experienced before. I was overcome with worry about my cancer, and I felt guilty about my life. I didn't feel like God cared about me. Now I feel peace like I have never known before, and there is a joy that makes me feel like laughing all the time. I did not know I could feel this good!" Martha gave Darrell and Mary big hugs as she wiped away her tears of joy. Bill even let Darrell and Mary hug him too.

"God Has Used You for My Miracle"

Darrell talked to them about the need to be baptized, and within two weeks they were at church preparing to be baptized. Darrell and Mary came to church early to help Bill and Martha. As Darrell helped Bill prepare for baptism, Bill mentioned Darrell's name. Then a man he had never seen approached them and asked excitedly, "Is your name Darrell? Are you the Darrell who led my mother-in-law to the Lord?!" Darrell said, "Yes, I guess I am that Darrell."

The man called out to a woman across the room, "Honey, this is Darrell! Here's the man we have been hearing so much about!" She ran over and gave Darrell a big hug, and introduced herself as Martha's daughter,

Meagan. Her husband's name was Matt. "I've been witnessing to my mother for more than ten years since I was saved, but she would not listen to me," she told Darrell. "Now God has used you for my miracle. Thank you so much for listening to the Lord, and meeting my mom's needs."

Then she explained, "When we heard both she and Bill had received the Lord, we couldn't believe it! After all these years, God answered our prayers. So we came all the way from Texas to see them get baptized. We both wanted to meet the man the Lord used to minister to my mother." Meagan said, "Thank you so much for all that you have done for her and for us!" Then she gave Darrell another hug. That night Meagan watched her mother being baptized, and she witnessed another life-changing miracle of the Care Ministry.

The Value of the Pursuit Ministry

Martha had a *relationship* with the church after she attended the first Sunday. She had a relationship of need. Because Darrell and Mary *pursued* her and met her need, she and Bill became part of the church. She was open to receive ministry from the church because she began a relationship with the church the first Sunday she attended. Martha gave many other churches the opportunity to experience the miracle she was waiting to experience, but they all refused the miracle. Without effective pursuit ministry, many miracles never take place.

How you minister to the visitor during the first week will determine whether he will come back. If visitors do come back a second time, there is a 56 percent chance that they will stay and receive your ministry. If visitors leave your church after the first visit, it is because they are not totally convinced that you care about them or love them.

Although about 15 percent won't like your church, you face a challenge for the 85 percent who are still undecided—you have to "earn the right" for them to return. One Sunday service does not make enough deposits in the visitors' life for them to decide to return. The church must develop a relationship with visitors and make deposits in the "emotional bank accounts" of those relationships.

For visitors coming to your church for the first time, the Sunday morning experience is a "withdrawal." Most churches view the Sunday morning service only as a method of making deposits, but actually, there is usually very little personal interaction in these situations. Most visitors feel distant from those conducting the service. The pastor is far away; the choir is far away. Nothing is up close and personal because the Sunday morning structure limits the type of personal contact necessary for them to know your heart. For them to return, you must deposit enough in their "emotional bank account" to motivate them to return. If you don't, they won't return. For most churches, the relationship ends when the visitors walk out the door.

Compassionate Pursuit Ministry

Most churches consider first-time attenders to be strangers. Since there is no relationship with them, they don't feel they have a responsibility to minister to their needs. They don't know how to make deposits in the relationship, so their follow-up does not meet the needs of the visitors. (Most of the time, we don't even consider their needs.) When we have compassion, we will discern their needs and serve them by helping them find a fulfilling relationship with Jesus.

The first problem in visitor follow-up is that most churches have wrong objectives for contacting visitors. They try to "sell" visitors on the superiority of their programs over other churches' programs. "We have a great choir, a great teen ministry, a great children's ministry, and a great Sunday school class!"

The fact is that visitors don't care about your church, or about you, because you are a stranger. You have to "earn the right" to minister to them by answering their questions: "Do you care about me? Do you care about my family? Do you care about my needs?" So how can we communicate to the visitors in a way that makes deposits in the relationship, and earns the right for them to return? The key is effective follow-up that is personal, loving, and caring.

Ineffective Staff-Driven Ministry

Most churches do not have personal ministry. Either the pastor, one of his staff, or volunteers will write letters or make the phone calls to visitors. If there are any visits, they are made by the staff. Church growth studies indicate it is 85 percent less effective for the visitor ministry to be staff-driven! Why? Visitors don't want a professional relationship; they want a *personal* relationship.

I interviewed an associate pastor responsible for the visitor ministry of a large church in the West. He said 4,500 visitors per year came through the doors. He personally called each visitor and invited them to his class, but only 40 out of 4,500 visitors came to his class! That is less than one percent. Staff-driven follow-up does not work.

Ineffective Layperson Follow-Up

Some churches expect a handful of lay volunteers to minister to literally hundreds and thousands of visitors each year, but they can't meet all the needs. What I found in most churches is that there are two or three individuals who like to talk to people who will call visitors on the phone. This strategy isn't employed because it is effective, but simply because the church does not have another strategy.

A Strange Call From a Stranger

My wife visited a church one time that had "strangers" calling the visitors. She told the unknown woman who called our home that she was looking for relationships in the church. When my wife asked the woman if she could meet her the next week, the "church lady" just said, "Oh, I'm in the foyer every Sunday, and you can meet me there" (but she didn't bother to say where she would be, what she looked like, or how they would meet).

Why was this woman so evasive? Was it because she was actually an unfriendly person? No. It was the wrong system. This poor woman was calling so many people every week that she did not have the emotional energy to meet everyone she called.

On the other hand, I was introduced to some visitors who had been attending a Care Group in one particular church for about a month. When I discovered they lived 45 minutes across town from where the Care Group was meeting, I remarked, "Isn't that a long way to drive to go to a Care Group?" Their reply revealed just how significant relational bonding is to meeting needs. They said, "No, it isn't! Forty-five minutes is not a long way to drive if *your needs are met*, if you are *developing friends*, and if you are *being loved!*" It was clear to me that if the group did not meet their needs, it could be held next door and they wouldn't go!

Seven Deposits in Pursuit Ministry

"The Pursuit Ministry" demonstrates to visitors by the action of your members how much your church really cares about them. It is proof that you want to serve them and meet their needs, and it communicates to them that your church is the church they have been looking for. The Care Ministry's "Pursuit Ministry" builds on the relational foundation begun on Sunday morning. What gives it even more dynamic impact is that now, for the first time, the visitors are actually receiving *personal deposits* from "friends" at church. The Care Team members are continuing to build the *relationship* established with the visitor on Sunday.

The Care Team members aren't trying to "touch" the visitor with superficial, impersonal contacts. Their goal for every post-church service contact is to motivate the first-time attenders to return to the church *so they can continue to minister to them* (not get them to become part of the church to meet *its* needs). The Care Team now has the relational foundation to make "Seven Deposits of Care" in the first-time attender.

The motivation of the Care Team is the greatest motivation of all: *love*. Everyone who contacts the visitor is an acquaintance, not a stranger, so each "contact" is transformed into a relational deposit of care and love.

1. *Sunday: The afternoon phone call.* A team member who has met the first-time attenders will make a "phone deposit" to communicate our concern for them, and to discover how the church met their needs that day. A series of questions are

asked about their visit, but the real importance of the call is the deposit that says, "Your being with us is important to us, and we value your input."

2. *Monday night: The "Cookie Crusade."* This simple "door encounter" allows a Care Team member to personally say, "I wanted to drop by to give you this gift of cookies. We want you to know we care about you, and your family is important to us."

Then the Care Team member will hand the visitor a "Free Gift Certificate" and say: "The pastor wants to give you a free gift when you come back, so bring this certificate to the hospitality table, and you will receive the free gift. It isn't a tape of a sermon, but something you can use every day." On the back of the card is the name of the Care Team member and the visitor.

When the visitor returns the card to the hospitality table the next service, you have accomplished three objectives. First, you have identified the second-time visitors. Second, you not only have the name of the second-time visitor, but also the Care Team member who ministered to them. The hospitality team finds the Care Team member, and tells him the visitor is back. Third, the Care Team member sits with the second-time visitor, and continues to build the relationship and provide personal ministry.

Some folks think it is very intrusive to go to someone's house. I was in Minneapolis conducting a seminar for pastors and leaders, when a woman stood up who was very upset that I would suggest going to someone's home for any reason.

Before I could answer her, the Care Ministry co-ordinator asked if he could answer the question. He said, "I had the same fears about this Cookie Crusade, especially in Minnesota; *you know how reserved we are up here.*" (Everyone laughed and nodded their heads.) Then he continued, "But we have found just the opposite response from our visitors. Instead of being offended, they are happy we are there! In fact, we are often invited into the home for fellowship!" Then I knew the Cookie Crusade would work anywhere.

Some of our greatest miracles happen in the homes of visitors, not in church buildings! One Care Team member showed up at a visitor's door armed with a load of cookies, only to find that the visitor was so despondent that he had a gun on the coffee table, and was contemplating suicide! That first-time attender got saved instead of committing suicide. Another Care Team member led five people to the Lord just by giving a gift of care. The miracles multiply when you get out of the church building and step into the lives of the people who come to your church with their needs. Don't prejudge the "cookie" deposit. Try it and watch God do miracles.

While church growth experts claim that going door to door doesn't work, the Jehovah's Witnesses have become the fastest growing religious sect in America by going from door to door! (They learned long ago that there are more needy people sitting in their homes than will ever attend a church in a decade!)

3. *Tuesday: Staff phone call.* You told the visitor the entire staff was going to pray for them on Tuesday. The staff ministers met the visitors on Sunday, so this call is a deposit, not a withdrawal.

4. *Wednesday: Personal letter from the pastor.* At the end of the pastor's letter is a handwritten postscript in which he tells them he is praying personally about the need they wrote down on the prayer request card (if applicable).

5. *Thursday: The Care Team leader calls.* He is not a stranger either, since he met the first-time attenders in church. Long before the visitors ever know he is the group leader, he is making deposits of care, building relationships, and meeting their needs. You want visitors to become part of the Care Group so they can have seven friends in six months, so you want them to feel good about the Care Team leader, and accept the invitation

to attend the group that comes later on. This deposit lays the groundwork of relationship for what occurs when the visitors return the next Sunday.

The conversation might sound like this: "Hello, Frank, this is Charlie from First Church. Do you remember me? We met after church when Bob introduced us. I want you to know we have been praying for you and your family every day this week." [Frank wrote on his prayer request card that his mother is in the hospital.] "How's your mother doing? Has she improved? Frank, would it be all right if some of us went to see her?" [Don't you know it would be a big deposit if some of the Care Team members briefly visited and prayed for Frank's mother in the hospital?]

Then the Care Team leader asks, "Frank, is there anything I can pray about with you?" Then he prays for the need. He doesn't invite Frank to the Care Group, and he doesn't invite him back to church. That is not his role. His goal is to make a deposit of care and love in Frank's heart. He concludes by saying, "Frank, I've enjoyed talking with you. Your family is important to us, and we will continue to pray for you and your mother. I hope to see you again soon and find out how things are going. God bless you."

6. *Friday: The Doorway Brochure.* On Friday, the visitor receives a brochure in the mail about the Care Ministry's specially designed noncommittal class geared to help him understand more about the church, its vision, and its values. It describes how the class will benefit visitors, and it motivates them to attend (ideally within a month of their first visit). The more they understand about the church, the easier it is for them to become a part.

7. *Saturday: The Care Team member's call.* Sometime on Saturday morning, the visitor will receive a call from the *friend* he met on Sunday morning. This is the same Care Team member who gave him the deposit of cookies on Monday. This is a "friend calling a friend" to ask him to come to church with him—not some stranger. It makes a deposit of friendship: "Hi, Frank. This is Bob from First Church. I want you to know my wife and I have been praying for you and your family every day this week. How's your mom doing in the hospital? You know, Charlie and I and some other folks went to see her, and prayed with her. She certainly is a wonderful person. She's proud of you too. It was a good visit. Charlie, my wife, and I would like to see you again, and we were wondering if you would want to come to church with us tomorrow? My wife could save some seats for us to sit together, and I could meet you in the

foyer. In fact, my wife was wondering if you and your family would enjoy coming over for Sunday dinner after church?"

This "call from a friend" takes place after a full week of caring deposits have been communicating how important the visitors and their needs are to us. This is the same *friend* from last week who gave them cookies. Now he has invited them to spend time together in church and over Sunday dinner. The first-time attender shouldn't feel like a "visitor" anymore!

It is impossible for *one person* to make the deposits necessary to motivate visitors to return. However, a *team* of Care ministers can make the deposits personally, and effectively communicate the care and love that makes the difference between the low retention rate you are probably experiencing right now and the dramatically high retention rate of the Care Ministry.

Second Sunday Strategy for Serving

Most churches don't have a clue what to do with second-time attenders, because they don't see the end from the beginning. In the Care Ministry, the second Sunday is devoted to building upon the relationships birthed on the first Sunday and the caring deposits made during the week. This strategy is not a scheme to manipulate; it is a plan to meet needs and to build friendships that will last a lifetime!

When Frank Visitor and his family sit down with Bob that second Sunday morning, the entire Care Team will make it a point to greet him and his family, as they did the previous week. Frank is being impacted by the entire Care Team *again*—he is receiving deposits from his future *Care Group*. Charlie, the Care Team leader, comes up and asks about Frank's mother; and Bob, Charlie, and Frank pray for her again. The Care Team members who went to the hospital also talk to Frank about her. By this time, Frank feels like the entire church is focused on his needs.

After church, Bob asks Frank, "Why don't you come to my Care Group this week?" Frank's first reaction is to think privately, "I am not going to go to a group of strangers!" But what he says is, "Oh, I'm too busy this week." (That might mean he is too busy watching TV or washing the car.) Bob just smiles and begins to point out all the members of the Care Group that Frank *already knows*! "Frank, did you know that Charlie is the leader of the Care Group?" Frank is surprised. The same person who called him Thursday and visited his mother in the hospital is also the Care Group leader.

Bob continues to point out everyone Frank met last week and that morning. "Frank, you know Jim and Sarah, and...." Suddenly Frank realizes he knows everyone in the Care Group already! All the obstacles of fear and uncertainty have been removed by the care and love of the Care Team. Now he wants to be with these people who have loved him so much, so Frank gladly accepts the invitation to attend Care Group. The Pursuit Ministry doesn't stop with the invitation, though. Bob says, "Frank, I could tell you where the Care Group meets, but why don't I just come by and pick you up instead?"

The love of God has even more power to draw people back to your church than the great worship, wonderful preaching, and anointed ministry found in the public meetings! Team Ministry will make any church grow because it *meets the heartfelt needs of visitors.* The secret of its great effectiveness is found in *relationships.*

Principles of Effective Pursuit Ministry

If the following six principles of effective Pursuit Ministry are applied, you will have the same type of results we have found in churches across America, Canada, England, Australia, the Bahamas, and Asia.

1. *Pursuit Ministry must be personal.* There is a big difference between personal and individual follow-up. "Personal follow-up" is when visitors know or have met the person who is contacting them. "Individual follow-up" is when a stranger calls a stranger. The Pursuit Ministry is "friends relating to friends."

2. *Pursuit Ministry must be focused on people's needs, not church programs.* What visitors really want to

know is: "Do you care about me? Will my needs be met?" The pursuit ministry must be need-driven, because it is a need-fulfillment ministry. Most churches handle follow-up like the Sunday school teacher who told me, "I can't believe I spent five minutes telling this lady about how great my Sunday school class was—without asking her one question about her or her needs!"

3. *Pursuit Ministry makes relational and emotional deposits.* If your church began a relationship with the visitors the day they walked through the door, then you must make relational deposits in the emotional bank account if you want them to come back.

4. *The Pursuit Ministry must be integrated into the assimilation process.* The "assimilation process" describes the systems and structures you have in place to lead visitors from a decision to attend your church to a sense of ownership in your church. The Pursuit Ministry must "see the end from the beginning." You are cultivating a *disciple*, not a church attender! How you follow up will determine what type of church member you will have.

5. *Pursuit Ministry must have the "WOW! factor."* Visitors who experience this type of caring pursuit will automatically respond by saying, "WOW!"

New Life Fellowship in Dallas, Texas, grew from 185 to almost 600 members in 18 months when its Care Ministry coordinator decided to make their usual "Cookie Crusade" into a "WOW event." Instead of sending just one person, George Wade sent the *entire Care Team* to visitors' homes to present gifts of cookies. Do you know what the visitors said when they saw 12 to 15 smiling people at their door? WOW! New Life became one of the fastest growing churches in America after putting the "WOW! factor" in their Pursuit Ministry.

6. *Pursuit Ministry must be repetitious.* A leadership axiom is: "All communication must be redundant and repetitive." That is especially true with the visitors. That is why you must have seven *deposits*, not touches. You are raising your level of personal involvement in their lives to go beyond "touching" to build a relationship of trust so you can *minister to them.* You are "earning the right" to become part of their life. Focus on their need and not the church. Do not sell the church; meet needs. Use repetition to communicate *care.* I am convinced you cannot tell someone too many times that you care for and love them!

The Pursuit Ministry Works

Our research has shown that the Pursuit Ministry is a determining factor in visitors returning to your church the second time. When they do return, you have a 56 percent chance of retaining them in your church. By implementing the Care Ministry strategies, systems, and structures, you will retain between 25 and 40 percent of your first-time attenders because your Pursuit Ministry will get over half of the visitors to return, and half of those will assimilate into the church!

Chapter 9

How to Make Disciples From Miracles

Down in Southwest Florida, in the Gulf of Mexico, there is a wily, sly fish called the "snook fish." They are hard to catch, but they are a great sport fish once you manage to hook them. John wasn't saved, but he attended church with his Christian wife anyway. He did not have any objections to going to church, but he had never received the Lord. Now one thing John loved to do was snook fish.

He attended a church where we had implemented the Care Ministry. There were some snook fishermen on the Care Team who ministered the same Sunday morning that John visited the church.

Jeff, the contact Care minister, discovered that John liked to fish, so he invited John to go snook fishing the following Saturday. He also invited George, another member of the Care team, so they could "team minister" to John.

As the three men were snook fishing off the bank, Jeff asked George how he got saved. Now John, the unsaved snook fisherman, was standing between them, and he couldn't help but listen to George's exciting testimony.

When George finished sharing his testimony, he threw the ball back into Jeff's court and asked him how he got saved! Guess who listened to Jeff's testimony? That's right, John was all ears. After Jeff finished sharing his testimony, *he asked John to share his testimony* about how the Lord came into his life. John said, "I don't think I have a testimony."

When Jeff asked, "Would you like to ask Jesus into your life right now?" John told him, "I've been wanting to for a long time, but I didn't have anyone to tell me how." Right there on the bank, John the "snook fisherman" received Jesus Christ as his Lord.

One of the exciting things about being on a Care Team is that you are not doing the ministry by yourself. It is team ministry. Care Groups are much more fun than fellowship groups because you have a team ministry that is reaching out to the unchurched and the unsaved to bond them into the group.

First Goal: Make Disciples

The number one mission of the Care Ministry is to make disciples. Most churches try to make visitors become members, but that is not biblical. Our mission is to fulfill the Great Commission of Christ by identifying hurting and needy first-time attenders, by meeting their needs, and by leading them into a fuller walk with the Lord.

People like John or "Frank and Sally Visitor" usually don't end up with seven friends in most churches in America. If they return to the church at all, they do it because they are determined to overcome obstacles in order to belong to a church. *Assimilation* is one of the biggest needs of the church today! I ask pastors all the time, "What is your structured assimilation process?" Most of the time, they either ask what I mean by "assimilation," or they say, "Oh yeah, we are working on that!" Some of the more candid pastors simply say, "That's why I'm talking to you."

Most churches do not see assimilation as a process from the first Sunday because they don't realize it takes *relationships* to lead visitors into functional membership. Most churches expect assimilation to take place in their small groups or in Sunday school classes. The problem is that these are really *maintenance structures*. Their primary purpose is to maintain the spiritual life of church members.

"Maintenance structures" are ineffective growth and assimilation structures for several important reasons:

1. *The leader believes that his primary job is to care for the people who come every week.* I developed the Care Ministry while I served as an associate pastor for a megachurch of 4,000. There were already 48 small groups meeting in homes, with the leaders assigned to contact the visitors. Some would and some would not, but in virtually every case, these contacts were not *deposits*. They were withdrawals because the leaders were strangers to the first-time attenders, and because they did not want to invest more than a phone call into the lives of visitors due to time limitations. Leaders of maintenance structures don't see assimilation as "their ministry."

2. *The people in these groups already have their friends.* Visitors attending these maintenance meetings will hit a wall of "relational saturation." It may be friendly, cordial, and even "Christian," but *it is still a wall*. The group members have already made friends in the group. They don't have the time or emotional energy to develop new friends, so they shut visitors out of their close relationships.

   This forces visitors to stand outside the relational wall and watch all the neat relationships and friendships of the group go on. They quickly realize they are not going to be invited in, so they will probably leave the group because it is not meeting their needs.

3. *The vision of the maintenance structure is to maintain, not to grow.* You can't have two visions for one structure. It will either maintain your church folk, or it will assimilate the visitors.

4. *There is no bridge between church and group.* Once a visitor leaves your church, there is an 85-90 percent chance they will never come back. Where do these poor souls go? I have discovered what happens to them: They fall into the "Abyss of No Return." "Where are Frank and Sally Visitor?" "Oh, I guess they fell into the abyss of no return. We'll never see them again!"

Some churches try to build a bridge from the church sanctuary to their small groups with church announcements: "We are proud to say we have geographic groups in your geographic area. Just call our church office and we will tell you where your nearest geographic group is." Meanwhile, the bewildered visitor is thinking, "What in the world is a *geographic group*? What does geography have to do with church? These are weird groups."

Once the "geographic group" announcement strategy has failed, some churches turn to "personal invitations" (by telephone, of course). The maintenance group leader is recruited to make an

"AT&T personal call" that sounds like this: "Hi, I don't know you, and you don't know me, but why don't you come to my group full of strangers?" The visitor is thinking, "Yeah, like I want to spend an entire evening with strangers who don't want to be my friend." In the end, he politely says, "I'm too busy."

His duty fulfilled, the maintenance group leader notes on his official "follow-up" form: "I called, but he is too busy." The pastor reads the report and feels good about his follow-up program. *I have one small but nagging question*: "How can anyone feel good about a task that is 90 percent ineffective?"

Assimilation Begins at the Door

In contrast to this, the Care Ministry assimilation process begins the first Sunday the visitor steps through the door of the church. Care Team members are determined to build a bridge of love and personal care that will carry visitors safely over the "abyss of no return" and into the loving environment of a Care Group. The most effective bridge in the church is the bridge of personal relationship and friendship in Christ.

Most Christians know they are to make disciples, but they do not know what a disciple looks like! It is very difficult to make something if you do not know what you are making. In the Care Ministry, you will be making an "I.I.D."

"I.I.D." stands for Initiated, Integrated Disciple. These three words define your ministry goals to make disciples for Jesus.

The first "I" is for "Initiated." We are initiating first-time attenders into the Kingdom of God, not the local church. Biblical initiation is found in Acts 2, when on the Day of Pentecost, Peter preached the first sermon. When the convicted crowd asked at the conclusion of his message, "Brethren, what shall we do?" Peter told them how to be initiated into the Kingdom of God. First, repent (that is our prayer of salvation), then be baptized, and finally, receive the gift of the Holy Spirit (see Acts 2:38). Those are the three keys into the Kingdom of God.

Your ministry with each first-time attender is to ensure they receive salvation and complete their initiation into the Kingdom of God by being baptized and receiving the gift of the Spirit. Most Christians believe that is the pastor's job description; biblically, it is the believer's ministry.

The Care Ministry goal is to restore the believer's ministry back to the believer. The most fulfilling experience a disciple of Jesus can have is to impart his faith to the heart of another person and see that individual receive Jesus into his heart!

The second "I" is for "Integrated." That means the visitor has become a functioning member of the local church. He must be related to be integrated. He has to be in a group of some sort, and he has to have a ministry.

The "D" is for "Disciple." This is a believer who knows the vision and the values of the local church. This knowledge is necessary because visitors need to know what they are committing themselves to be and do, and the vision and values define that.

You Are an "I.I.D.-Maker"

Every first-time attender must become an I.I.D. in order for your ministry to become complete. You are an "I.I.D.-maker." That is your goal for the ministry and for your team, and it is done through bridge building. Genuine bridge building can only be done by a Care Team that sees the end from the beginning. They must have a fresh vision of their ministry and a clear understanding of the needs of the visitor. They need to know the Bible-based ministry strategy, systems, and structures that equip the church and the believer to fulfill the ministry.

One Vision, Two Purposes

The Care Group fulfills *two purposes* for *one vision*: (a) to make and multiply disciples and (b) to maintain and train the Care Team. As we noted earlier, Care Groups consist of believers who are fulfilling the "work of the ministry" and *former* visitors who are receiving their ministry through relationship. *The Care Group is a vision-driven small group!*

Every member of the Care Team has a goal of making disciples of Frank and Sally Visitor. It is a "team" ministry. Frank and Sally don't have to wait six months to have seven friends. The entire Care Team has already become their friends before they ever attend a Care Group meeting! The team is dedicated to helping Frank and Sally become part of their group. This is accomplished through the Care Team's fivefold commitment to their twofold mission.

Fivefold Commitment to the Care Group Mission

1. *To befriend the visitors.* The Care Team members know visitors need seven friends in six months, and it is their ministry objective to personally become genuine friends.

2. *To love the visitors.* Each Care Team minister knows each visitor needs to be accepted, to belong, to feel needed, and to feel important (or appreciated). (These are the four "universal heartfelt needs" of visitors described in Chapter 3.)

3. *To help the visitors bond to the Care Group.* People do not "plug into" a church. Visitors are not machines; they are people who need to bond to other people in a church *through relationships.* The Care Team wants visitors to feel bonded to their group.

4. *To meet the needs of the visitors.* Need-fulfillment is the responsibility of the entire team. The team already knows the visitors' needs, because they have personally talked with and prayed for them all along.

5. *To make disciples of the visitors.* The Care Team works together to make sure visitors are saved, baptized, and assimilated into the church. The Care Team ministry does not conclude until the visitor is bonded to the Care Group. Once this happens, the Care Team members release the new members to the bonding of the Care Group and they begin to disciple new visitors. The ultimate goal is for the new members of the Care Group to grow and join the Care Team.

How does this work? Let's say that I go up to Frank Visitor and say, "Hey, Frank. We've got a bunch of crazy people over in this group and they love you. You know some of them already, because we went fishing together. [He likes snook fishing too.] You even know the leader, because he called you and prayed with you over the phone. We meet and fellowship every week, and we love and encourage each other. Why don't you come?" So Frank says, "Okay."

They Need Seven Friends

So I go by and pick up Frank and his wife, Sally, to take them to the Care Group. I'll take them to the

Group meeting three times to make sure they are properly bonded. Now, how many friends do Frank and Sally need? They need seven friends in six months or what happens? Yes, Frank and Sally are "out the door." That is why we have to get that relational bonding going. Frank and Sally need seven friends. Do they have to wait six months to get seven friends? No. You have a whole team of people who are committed to being their friends and loving them. They know this couple needs the bonds of love, so they are all committed to loving them and seeing them bond to the group where they will feel accepted, appreciated, and needed, and have a sense of belonging. Everyone in the Care Group wants to meet their four universal needs, and they are committed to their being bonded into the group and becoming disciples of Jesus.

The fruit of this kind of loving commitment is the fulfillment of the mission. Frank and Sally are now a part of the church, and they are living a different kind of lifestyle. They are not just "Sunday morning church attenders," but praise God, they are disciples of Jesus! They belong to a caring group of people who are all committed to mutual success, for they know they can't fulfill their twofold mission by themselves. They are now a part of a team that has a fivefold commitment to their twofold mission. Frank and Sally are ready to step into the anointed ministry of the Care Team and help bring in the harvest for Christ.

Second Goal: Multiply the Group

The second goal is to multiply the group. When the group gets to about 16 to 18 people, it will multiply. Care Groups grow and multiply by bonding. To be the structure for bonding, Care Team members must become a "bridge" from the Sunday morning service to the Care Groups.

How are the visitors going to progress from a one-dimensional Sunday morning meeting to the Care Groups? What's the bridge from the structure of Sunday morning to the structure of the group? This is where you fit into the picture.

The most effective bridge over the abyss between church and group is a personal relationship between you and the first-time attender. You become the bridge by personally taking the visitor to the Care Group three times. You will also take the visitor to the "Doorway class," or your introductory class, three times. Your personal relationship will motivate him to attend the group because you have lowered the obstacles to attending it through your personal involvement and care.

Monte and Pam Find a Home

Monte and Pam attended a church and were overwhelmed by the Care Team members' attention and love. This couple had never experienced this kind of care in a church before. Drew and Julie, a couple on the

Care Team, became their friends and prayed with them about their upcoming move to the city and the new careers they were entering. Pam had not found a job yet, and they needed both incomes to make ends meet. If she didn't find a job, they were going to have "more month at the end of the money." Drew and Julie's prayer gave Monte and Pam the faith to believe God was going to bless them soon.

They left church that day excited about the personal ministry they had received, but they weren't really sure if this was the right church. The very next night, Drew showed up at their door with some cookies. They invited him in, and they prayed again for Pam's interviews. The care continued throughout that week, as Monte and Pam discovered the church staff was also praying for her job, and an entire prayer team had dedicated the week to pray for her! By the time she went for the interview, she was confident the Lord was favoring her, and she got the job!

When Drew called on Saturday and invited them back to church, they couldn't wait to tell him how God had answered everyone's prayers, and to say how thankful they were to the church for all the people who were praying for them. Drew told them the Care Team would love to hear how God had blessed them, and asked them to come to church so they could share the good news themselves.

Feeling More Comfortable

Monte and Pam met Drew and Julie at church on Sunday morning, and sat with them. They were greeted by the entire Care Team, the same people they had met and talked with the week before. They were feeling much more comfortable in church this week.

When the couple told everyone about how God had already answered their prayers, and how Pam had landed the job, everyone got excited. Pam told Drew, "It is so much fun coming to church and having so many people sharing the joy of me getting my job. And this is only our second Sunday here!"

After church, Drew invited them to the Care Group. Monte told him, "We would like to, but we are too busy this week." Drew smiled, because that is what I told him the visitors would say. Then he asked them if they knew the leader of the Care Group, Jim. They remembered a "Jim" who had called them the week before and had prayed with them about Pam's job interview the night before it took place. His prayer really helped. Monte asked, "*Jim* is the leader of the group?" When Drew told him it was the same person, Monte and Pam's attitude immediately changed.

Then Drew began to point out all the people they already knew who were in the group, people who had prayed and cared about them. Monte and Pam actually began to smile when they realized they would be with people who cared personally for them.

"It Would Be Fun"

Drew then suggested, "Monte, instead of me telling you where the group meets, why don't Julie and I just come by and pick you up?" Monte responded with peace in his voice, "I'd like that. Would you, Pam?" She said, "Yes, it would be fun to be with these folks."

At the Care Group that week, Monte told everyone, "Pam and I were thinking of visiting another, larger church this week because we heard they had great ministries, but *we have found what we were looking for.* We have found more than a 'church home'; we have found people who love us and care about us. When we left our church back home, we didn't think we would ever find the kind of love we had there, but we were wrong. Thanks for loving us, for caring for us, for praying for us, and for wanting us. We're home."

Then Jim said, "Monte, we have a tradition in our group to pray for the people who attend our group for the first time. Would it be all right if we prayed for you and Pam right now?" Monte said, "Since you've been praying for us all week, I want you to pray for us!"

Jim placed a couple of chairs in the center of the room, and Monte and Pam sat in them while the group gathered around to pray for them. Monte and Pam held hands, and you could see the excitement in Pam's eyes as she looked at Monte. After the group prayed for them, Pam was crying. She said, "I've been afraid ever since we knew we had to move that we would not find somebody who would be our friends and love us. I've really been afraid of being all alone here, but I'm not afraid any longer." Everyone in the group hugged them, and told them they loved them.

The Doorway Class

Many times visitors may attend church for months and never discover the "door" into the life and ministry of that church. We have designed a simple four-week class to help visitors understand the vision and values of the church, the responsibilities of a member, the blessings of membership, and the various ministry involvement opportunities for them.

We have especially designed this class to help visitors come to the place of having "ownership" of the church. We want you to take them to the class three times to make sure that bonding takes place. By personally taking them to the class all three times, you can make sure that they begin to know other people, and that they know the pastor. This will make them feel comfortable enough to go to the class on their own in the fourth week. Why? Because you've broken down the barriers and obstacles to their involvement.

The Mission of the Meeting

We also want you to take visitors to Care Group three times so the *whole Care Team* can focus in on these folks. They are the mission of the meeting and the reason the Care Groups exist! Our fellowship has a two-fold mission, and we're going to fellowship together and meet each other's needs so we can fulfill that mission. But when "first-time attenders" come into the group, they're the reason we're here, so the whole team is committed to bonding with each "first-time attender" who comes to the group.

Not Just a Theory

The Care Ministry is not just a theory, it is *working* in churches across America, England, and Canada! It is transforming churches, believers, and communities around the world! The "secret" of its great effectiveness is simple: *Needs are being met supernaturally by the people of God.* God's people are seeking divine appointments as members of Care Teams. They understand that visitors aren't visitors; they are miracles disguised as needs. They are committed to pursuing, loving, and meeting the needs of first-time attenders until they become disciples of Jesus Christ! Are you ready to join the great last days army of God?

9412 Delmar
Prairie Village, KS 66207

The material in this book was originally developed for seminars that train members of the local church to fulfill the ministry. Today there are several facilitators who implement the Care Ministry into local churches throughout the United States. The Care Ministry seminar will expand the local ministry from the involvement of a few individuals to 20 percent of the church in team ministry. A local church's effectiveness with this ministry is significantly enhanced by having the seminar training.

Weekend Seminar

The seminar consists of three levels of ministry training. On Saturday night team leaders have three hours of leadership training. On Sunday the facilitator preaches and recruits 20 percent of the congregation with a passion for ministry and a vision for the growth of the church. That Sunday night the training for the members begins with three 45-minute training sessions. Then on Monday night the training continues with two or more sessions. On Monday morning there is consultation for the pastoral staff.

Call **1-800-769-GROW** for a free video or a visitor ministry needs analysis.